For Whom Did Christ Die?

FOR WHOM DID CHRIST DIE?

A STUDY OF THE DIVINE DESIGN OF THE ATONEMENT

by

R. B. Kuiper

Professor Emeritus of Practical Theology
Westminster Theological Seminary
President Emeritus of Calvin Seminary

Wipf and Stock Publishers
EUGENE, OREGON

Wipf and Stock Publishers
199 West 8th Avenue, Suite 3
Eugene, Oregon 97401

For Whom Did Christ Die?
A Study of the Divine Design of the Atonement
By Kuiper, R. B.

ISBN: 1-59244-409-1
Publication date 11/5/2003
Previously published by Wm. B. Eerdmans Publishing Co., 1959

INTRODUCTION

Within what is loosely called Protestantism there are three views concerning the divine design of the atonement in relation to the salvation of men. They may be denominated unrestricted universalism, inconsistent universalism, and particularism. The first is held by the Universalist Church, by numerous liberals scattered throughout many denominations and by a limited number of such as would be known as theological conservatives. The second is held by Arminians and, with certain variations, by the Lutheran churches. The universalism of Karl Barth, although differing substantially from that of Arminianism, is also inconsistent. The third is held by those churches and persons that adhere uncompromisingly to historic Calvinism. Briefly put, the first view is that God designed by the atonement to save all men and that in consequence all men are saved; the second is that God designed by the atonement to save all men but that somehow not all are saved; the third is that God designed by the atonement to save only the elect and that in consequence all the elect, and they alone, are saved.

Firmly convinced that only the last named of these views is Scriptural, I wish to uphold it in contradistinction to the other two.

It is my aim to do more than that.

The particular atonement is one of the so-called five points of Calvinism, the other four being unconditional election, total depravity, irresistible grace, and the perseverance or preservation of the saints. Of the five the particular atonement is perhaps the least popular.

It is unpopular for the same reason that makes the Reformed doctrine of salvation unpopular in all its parts. Salvation by the sovereign grace of God, and by that grace alone, is the very heart of the Reformed faith. It tells man that salvation belongs exclusively to the Lord and that, apart from the grace of God working in him both to will and to do, he can contribute precisely nothing to it. By insisting that God receives all the honor for man's salvation and that he himself receives none, it humiliates man as does no other teaching of salvation. In the words of Charles Haddon Spurgeon: "If there be but one stitch in the celestial garment of our righteousness which we ourselves are to put in, we are lost." Of that exceedingly unpopular truth the doctrine of the particular atonement is an integral part.

There is, I fear, an additional reason of quite another kind for the unpopularity of the doctrine of the particular atonement. It lies not in Calvinism but in Calvinists, not in the Reformed faith but in some of its teachers; and it is not complimentary to them. Seldom does one hear from a Reformed pulpit an accurate statement of this doctrine. It is not at all unusual for Reformed preachers, in attempting to state it, to content themselves with saying that Christ died only for the elect. But that presentation requires both explanation and amplification. By itself it falls short of doing justice either to the Scriptural data bearing on the matter or to its historic formulation in the creeds of the Reformed and Presbyterian churches and the writings of the ablest Reformed theologians. In consequence, serious-minded hearers who have at least a superficial acquaintance with those passages of Scripture which bear on the scope of the atonement and who are not completely ignorant of the teaching on this subject by the church's confessions and theologians, are left dissatisfied and confused.

It is a matter, not only of theoretical import, but also of the greatest practical necessity, that the doctrine of the so-called limited atonement be set forth in the full light of the teaching of the Word of God. What follows constitutes an attempt in that direction. *The Divine Design of the Atonement* is our theme. It will be shown that God's design in the atonement was indeed in a most real sense particular. It will also be shown that God's design in the atonement was in a no less real sense universal.

This study will be based on the Bible as the one and only infallible rule of faith. In that respect my approach will differ from that of James Denney in his well-known and in evangelical circles justly famous *The Death of Christ* and *The Atonement and the Modern Mind.* He professes to prize Scripture because of the truth he finds in it. I accept the teachings of Scripture as truth because I believe Scripture to be the Word of God. Significant as this difference is, it is evident that as a matter of fact Denney did base his statement of the atonement largely, if not wholly, on Holy Writ. Incidentally it may be remarked that on the precise theme of this study Denney has little to say. He did not intend to set forth the doctrine of the atonement in full, and that aspect of the atonement here presented did not lie at the focal point of his attention.

I wish to thank Dr. F. H. Klooster, Associate Professor of Systematic Theology at Calvin Seminary, for reading my manuscript and offering valuable suggestions for its improvement. It hardly needs to be said that I alone am responsible for the chapters that follow.

I am grateful to the Presbyterian and Reformed Publishing Company for permission to quote from Benjamin B. Warfield's *Biblical Doctrines* and *Studies in Theology;* to Dr. Cornelius Van Til for permission to quote from his monograph on *Common Grace*; to Harper and Brothers for permission to quote from Nels F.S. Ferre's *The Christian Understanding of God*; to the Trustees under the will of J. Gresham Machen for permission to quote from J. Gresham Machen's *The Christian View of Man;* to the Wm. B. Eerdmans Publishing Company for permission to quote from Louis Berkhof's *Systematic Theology* and *Vicarious Atonement through Christ,* J. Gresham Machen's *God Transcendent and Other Sermons,* Loraine Boettner's *Studies in Theology,* the English translation of G. C. Berkouwer's *De Triomf der Genade in de Theologie van Karl Barth,* and the 1937 edition of *The International Standard Bible Encyclopaedia;* to the New York World-Telegram Corporation for permission to quote from the 1958 *World Almanac*: and to the National Council of the Churches of Christ in the United States of America, Division of Christian Education, for permission to quote from the Revised Standard Verson of the Bible, copyrighted 1946 and 1952. Such Biblical quotations are identified in the text.

In presenting this study I have in mind not only the theologian but also the preacher — if indeed the two may be differentiated — and the man in the pew as well as the occupant of the pulpit.

It may be deemed appropriate for this volume to come from the press in the year 1959, the 450th anniversary of the birth of John Calvin.

R. B. KUIPER

CONTENTS

Introduction

ONE: UNRESTRICTED UNIVERSALISM 11

TWO: ARMINIAN UNIVERSALISM 24

THREE: BARTHIAN UNIVERSALISM 44

FOUR: SCRIPTURAL PARTICULARISM 62

FIVE: SCRIPTURAL UNIVERSALISM 78

Index of Proper Names 101

Index of Scripture Passages 103

CHAPTER ONE

UNRESTRICTED UNIVERSALISM

Unrestricted Universalism in the History of Doctrine

The notion of the ultimate salvation of all men was first carried from paganism into Christianity by Clement of Alexandria, who died between 211 and 216, and his pupil Origen. With the Platonic doctrine of the pre-existence of human souls as his starting point, Origen taught that they are clothed with bodies to the ends of education and discipline and that the outcome of that process is unavoidably salutary. He went much farther and taught the salvation of even the fallen angels. In the fourth century both Gregory of Nazianzus and Gregory of Nyssa taught universal salvation. The former drew a universalistic conclusion from his attempt to solve the problem of sin. According to him God permitted sin and its consequences to enter the world only because of the divine foreknowledge that in the end all men would be saved. Although medieval theology, notably in the West, was in the main opposed to universalism, John Scotus Erigena, of the ninth century, taught a universal atonement.

In the days of the Protestant Reformation there were those who taught that God had elected all to eternal life and that, therefore, the salvation of all was certain. In 1567 a synod held at Debreczen drew up a *Summa Confessionis et Conclusionum* which spoke of these as *holopraedestinarii* and condemned their teaching. At no time since have there lacked within the fold of Protestantism those who taught universal salvation through the accomplished work of Christ. F. W. Schleiermacher, often called the father of present-day theological liberalism, was a universalist. More recent

European examples are the eminent Scottish theologians William Hastie of the University of Glasgow and William P. Paterson of the University of Edinburgh.

In America, before the time of organized universalism, there were advocates of this faith in many denominations, among them William Smith, founder of the University of Pennsylvania and for many years president of the general convention of the Protestant Episcopal Church, and such leading Congregationalists as Charles Chauncy and Jonathan Mayhew. Unitarianism and Swedenborgianism, as well as Christian Science, teach a universal salvation. The Universalist Church of America was founded in 1779 at Gloucester, Massachusetts. In 1803 its general convention, assembled at Winchester, New Hampshire, drew up a Profession of Belief containing the article: "We believe that there is one God, whose nature is Love . . . . and who will finally restore the whole family of mankind to holiness and happiness,"[1] and the general convention of 1899 included in the "essential principles," the acceptance of which is a condition of fellowship, "the final harmony of all souls with God."[2] According to the 1958 *World Almanac*[3] the Universalist Church comprises 388 congregations and a membership of 70,519. Although the denomination has never flourished, adherents of the universalist faith are numerous in some churches, and there is at least a scattering of them in a great many churches. Generally speaking, the more liberal a church is in its theology, the more numerous are universalists in its membership.

At the present time there is in process an extremely vigorous resurgence of outright universalism. Not only do Jehovah's Witnesses and several other sects teach a second probation and deny eternal suffering; influential churchmen in many lands and various denominations are proclaiming aloud the ultimate salvation of all men.

1. Article II.
2. A 5.
3. Published by *The New York World-Telegram and The Sun.*

Prominent among British advocates of universalism are such well-known and highly reputed scholars as C. H. Dodd, J. A. T. Robinson and H. H. Farmer. Robinson concluded an article "Universalism — Is It Heretical?" in *The Scottish Journal of Theology* with the asseveration: "Christ, in Origen's old words, remains on the cross as long as one sinner remains in hell. This is not a speculation: it is a statement grounded in the very necessity of God's nature. In a universe of love there can be no heaven which tolerates a chamber of horrors, no hell for any, which does not at the same time make it hell for God. He cannot endure that — for that would be the final mockery of his nature — and he *will* not."[4]

As might be expected, universalism is not without exponents in Germany and Switzerland. Time and again in the religious literature of our day Karl Barth is spoken of as a universalist. However, as will be pointed out subsequently in this discussion, his universalism is of the inconsistent type. Barth knows full well that the Bible teaches the everlasting damnation of some, and this knowledge evidently holds him in check. In 1950 Wilhelm Michaelis published his *Universal Redemption: The Good News of the Grace of God,* and in that volume he upholds an unqualified universalism. It must be said to his credit that, unlike most outright universalists, he seeks to substantiate his position by exegesis of Holy Scripture.

Of the numerous American theologians who insist on the ultimate salvation of all men, perhaps the most outstanding is Nels F. S. Ferre, who was born in Sweden but received his education in these United States and has achieved fame by his writings as well as the teaching of philosophy and religion at Andover Newton Theological School and the Vanderbilt University School of Religion. He deems it inconceivable that a God of absolute sovereignty, perfect justice, and infinite love would permit anyone to perish everlastingly. In *The Christian Understanding of God* Ferre

4. II, p. 155.

asserts that by condemning Origen for his denial of eternal hell "the Church judged itself the proclaimer of another than the Christian Gospel." He goes on to say: "If eternal hell is real, love is eternally frustrated and heaven is a place of mourning and concern for the lost. Such joy and such grief cannot go together. There can be no psychiatric split personality for the real lovers of God and surely not for God Himself. That is the reason that heaven can be heaven only when it has emptied hell, as surely as love is love and God is God. God cannot be faithless to Himself no matter how faithless we are; and His is the power, the kingdom and the glory."[5] With increasing frequency American pastors and professors of theology, many of them in denominations the doctrinal standards of which confess unmistakably the everlasting suffering of unbelievers, are boldly denouncing that doctrine from their pulpits and in their classrooms as utterly unworthy of a God whose essence is love.

It goes altogether without saying that not all thorough-going universalists subscribe to the Scriptural interpretation of the atonement as substitutionary. Many repudiate with utmost vigor any such view of the atonement. It is no exaggeration to assert that more than a few universalists abhor the Scriptural teaching that the death of Christ was a vicarious sacrifice for the expiation of sin by the satisfaction of divine justice. Yet the great majority of them, perhaps even all of them, believe that in one way or another, "God was in Christ reconciling the world unto himself" (II Cor. 5:19). In other words, their teaching of universal salvation involves a universalistic conception of the atonement.

Unrestricted Universalism in the Light of Scripture

Many weighty objections have been raised against the doctrine of the ultimate salvation of all men. It has been argued that this teaching cannot but take the edge off evangelistic effort and destroy the urgency of preaching to the

5. Harper & Brothers, New York, 1951, pp. 236f.

unsaved. The validity of that argument is undeniable. He who is convinced that sooner or later all men will enter upon a state of unending bliss cannot consistently urge sinners to respond to the love of God by believing on the gift of His love, even His only-begotten Son, on penalty of being banished everlastingly from communion with God; nor can he preach passionately on the Pauline plea: "Now then we are ambassadors for Christ, as though God did beseech you by us: we pray you in Christ's stead, be ye reconciled to God" (II Cor. 5:20). It has been argued that the universalist is guilty of a false analogy in patterning God after himself, equating divine love with human love and deducing from the consideration that he himself would not sentence any human being, no matter how perverse, to eternal suffering that neither is God capable of such retribution. That objection, too, is unanswerable. Again, the universalist has been charged with rationalism, not in every instance in the sense that he completely rejects Scripture as God's self-revelation, but at least in the sense that he *interprets* the Word of God rationalistically. That he does that very thing permits of no doubt, for in the interest of what he regards as logical consistency he stresses certain teachings of Scripture concerning the nature of God to the detriment, and even denial, of other equally clear teachings of Scripture on the same subject. And it may well be remarked here that precisely that type of rationalism has in the course of history become the fruitful mother of a veritable host of heresies.

However, all the aforenamed arguments, together with any other valid argument that can be brought against unrestricted universalism, add up to precisely one. It is that the Word of God contradicts that teaching.

From the viewpoint of Scripture it is difficult to take unqualified universalism seriously. One obvious reason is that universalists by and large do not take Scripture seriously. This is true particularly of those of recent date. There are, to be sure, a few notable exceptions, but the rule obtains.

Very few universalists regard the Bible as the infallible Word of God. Therefore hardly any are at all zealous to substantiate their theology with Scripture. A concerted attempt to base one's theology on Scripture is customarily berated as "biblicism." Admittedly universalist doctrine is derived, not so much from the Bible as from the reason and moral sense of its exponents. Because they cannot conceive of a God who would sentence certain of His creatures to eternal perdition and find it impossible to respect such a God, they conclude that God simply cannot do such a thing. Especially do they insist that the perfection of the divine *love* precludes everlasting punishment, whatever the Bible may say to the contrary notwithstanding. Not even universalist William P. Paterson, an avowed Calvinist, bowed unreservedly before the plain teaching of the Word of God, but forced upon it a rationalistic interpretation, when he said: "It is in the power of God, in virtue of the principle of irresistible grace, to save even the worst, and if nevertheless there is a part of the human race which is consigned to everlasting punishment, it seems to be only explicable on the assumption that the divine love is not perfect, because it is not an all-embracing and untiring love."[6]

Another reason why it is difficult, impossible even, from the viewpoint of Scripture to take unqualified universalism seriously is that Scripture contradicts it so patently, so frequently, and so emphatically. So unmistakably is the eternal punishment of the wicked taught in Scripture that even he who runs may read. It is especially prominent in the words of the Lord Jesus. He who rejects it presumes to be more merciful than the Son of God, than divine love incarnate. Repeatedly He spoke of the place "where their worm dieth not and the fire is not quenched" (Mark 9:44-48). He admonished: "Be not afraid of them that kill the body, and after that have no more that they can do. But I will forewarn you whom ye shall fear: Fear him which after he hath killed hath power to cast into hell" (Luke 12:4, 5). In the par-

6. *The Rule of Faith,* London and New York, 1912, p. 313.

able of the tares He did not teach that the tares will eventually become wheat, but, contrariwise, that "in the end of the world" the angels will gather them and "cast them into a furnace of fire" (Matt. 13:40-42). And in the parable of the net He taught that, as bad fish are cast away, "so shall it be at the end of the world: the angels shall come forth and sever the wicked from among the just, and shall cast them into the furnace of fire: there shall be wailing and gnashing of teeth" (Matt. 13:48-50). When Christ said: "Whosoever speaketh a word against the Son of man, it shall be forgiven him; but whosoever speaketh against the Holy Ghost, it shall not be forgiven him, neither in this world, neither in the world to come" (Matt. 12:32), He did not imply that sins against the Son of man can be forgiven in the age to come, but He stressed the absolutely unpardonable character of the sin against the Holy Ghost. On the day of judgment the Judge will say to the goats: "Depart from me, ye cursed, into everlasting fire prepared for the devil and his angels" (Matt. 25:41). Their suffering is to be as interminable as that of the evil spirits. And when the righteous enter upon "life eternal," these shall go into "everlasting punishment" (Matt. 25:46). Significantly the same Greek adjective[7] is here used to describe the future life of the saved and the future punishment of the lost. The latter will be as eternal as the former. The teaching of the eternal punishment of the wicked is by no means restricted to the words of Christ. To name but a few other instances, the apostle Paul spoke of

7. The contention that *aiõnios* may in this context mean something less than *everlasting* has not the slightest validity. While the noun *aiõn* often denotes an age which is not endless, the adjective occurs in the New Testament in the following three senses only: *without beginning or end, without beginning, without end.* In the first sense it is used of God in Rom. 16:26. It occurs in the second sense, for example, in II Tim. 1:9, where mention is made of the calling of God's own *pro chronõn aiõniõn* or *from eternity.* In Matt. 25:41, 46 it can only mean *without end, never to cease, everlasting.* See Thayer's *Greek English Lexicon of the New Testament* under *aiõnios.* Kittel's *Theologisches Wörterbuch zum Neuen Testament* also insists that *aiõnios* describes the "punishment" of Matt. 25:46, as well as the "fire" of Matt. 18:8; 25:41; Jude: 7, and the "destruction" of II Thess. 1:9, as "niemals aufhörend, endlos."

"the everlasting destruction from the presence of the Lord and from the glory of his power" of them "that obey not the gospel of our Lord Jesus Christ (II Thess. 1:8, 9); and the apostle of love recorded in his Gospel the decisive words of John the Baptist: "He that believeth on the Son hath everlasting life: and he that believeth not the Son shall not see life; but the wrath of God abideth on him" (John 3:36) and asserted in the Apocalypse that the smoke of the torment of those who worship the beast and his image "ascendeth up for ever and ever" (Rev. 14:11).

There are indeed certain passages of Scripture to which universalists like to appeal in support of the ultimate salvation of all men, but these passages can be construed as lending support to that teaching only if they are isolated both from their immediate context and from the system of doctrine that is taught in Scripture, the *regula Scripturae*. Some of the most favored of these passages will be considered.

Ephesians 1:10 says that it is the purpose of God to "gather together in one," to bring into one harmonious whole, "all things in Christ, both which are in heaven and which are on earth"; and in Colossians 1:19, 20 it is asserted that it pleased the Father, "having made peace through the blood of the cross, by him to reconcile all things unto himself . . . whether they be things in earth or things in heaven." On these passages Charles Hodge comments: "The question is, who, or what are the all, who are to be reconciled unto God? This question must be answered by a reference to the nature of the thing spoken of, and to the analogy of Scripture. It cannot mean absolutely 'all things,' the whole universe, including sun, moon, and stars, for they are not susceptible of reconciliation to God. For the same reason it cannot mean all sensitive creatures, including irrational animals. Nor can it mean all rational creatures, including the holy angels; for they do not need reconciliation. Nor can it mean all fallen rational creatures, for it is expressly taught, Hebrews 2:16, that Christ did not come to redeem fallen angels. Nor can it mean all men, for the Bible teaches elsewhere that all men are not reconciled to God; and Scripture cannot contradict Scripture; for that would be for God to contradict Himself. The 'all' intended is the 'all' spoken of in the context, the whole body of the people of God, all the objects of redemption."[8] As a matter of fact, in the immediate context of both of these passages the apostle deals unmistakably with the members of Christ's church. If, however, it be objected, as likely it must, that Hodge's argumentation is unsatisfactory in that it fails to do justice to the neuter "all things," then it becomes no less certain that the passages under consideration do not teach the ultimate salvation of all men. The text tells us that *the universe* will be reconciled to God. But does that imply that every rational creature in the universe will be reconciled to God? The answer must be an unequivocal negative. Not only is Hodge correct in arguing that the plain teaching of Scripture elsewhere forbids the interpretation that the fallen angels and all fallen men will share in the final reconciliation, but the Word of God teaches emphatically that the reconciliation of the universe to God will be effected in part precisely by the banishment of God's enemies. In accord with Scripture is Meyer's statement: "Through the Parousia the reconciliation of the whole which has been effected in Christ will reach its consummation, when the unbelieving portion of mankind will be separated and consigned to Gehenna, the whole creation in virtue of the Palingenesia will be transformed into its original perfection, and the new heaven and the new earth will be constituted as the dwelling of righteousness and of the glory of the children of God; while the demoniac portion of the angelic world will be removed from the sphere of the new world, and cast into hell. Accordingly, in the whole creation there will no longer be anything alienated from God and object of His hostility, but 'all things' will be in harmony and reconciled with Him; and God

8. *Systematic Theology,* London and Edinburgh, 1878, III, 871.

Himself, to whom Christ gives back the regency which He has hitherto exercised, will become the only Ruler and All in All."[9]

Romans 5:18 and I Corinthians 15:22 are usually regarded as parallel passages. That may well be done if only it be remembered that the former speaks of the benefit of justification through Christ, the latter of the benefit of the resurrection of the body with Christ. Both of these benefits are spoken of as in a sense universal. Says Romans 5:18, "As by the offense of one, judgment came upon all men to condemnation; even so by the righteousness of one, the free gift came upon all men unto justification of life." And I Corinthians 15:22 reads: "For as in Adam all die, even so in Christ shall all be made alive." How obviously the meaning of "all" in both of these passages is restricted by the context. As for the Corinthian passage, immediately after saying: "in Christ shall all be made alive," Paul proceeds: "But every man in his own order: Christ the firstfruits; afterward they that are Christ's at his coming." Clearly the "all" of this passage are not all men but "they that are Christ's." In like manner the "all" of the Romans passage are all that are in Christ. All that are in Christ are here contrasted with all that are in Adam. And it goes without saying that only believers are in Christ. That is the indisputable teaching of all the Pauline epistles and of the whole Bible.

Says F. L. Godet on the "all" of I Corinthians 15:22, "Most commentators (Augustine, Bengel, Rueckert, Hofmann, Holsten, Beet, Edwards, etc.) think that we must understand a self-evident condition, that of faith: 'As in Adam all men die, so in Christ shall all (believers) be made alive.' This limitation of the meaning of the second 'all' seems at first sight very arbitrary, in view of the absolute meaning of the first. But we shall get reconciled to this interpretation if we take account of Hofmann's observation that *to be made*

9. *Meyer's Commentary on the New Testament*, New York and London, 1885, on Col. 1:20.

alive[10] is a more limited idea than *to be raised.*[11] For this second term applies in general to all who shall live again, even to perish, whereas the first applies to the complete gift of perfect life (Rom. 8:11). The limitation of the subject can therefore naturally proceed from the special meaning of the verb itself. 'The two *alls* embrace those only to whom each of the two powers extends' (Hofmann). Moreover, it should be remembered that Christ can hardly be regarded as the *first-fruits* of the damned who are raised again, and verse 23, which continues the development begun in verse 20, evidently takes account only of believers."[12] And William G. T. Shedd identifies "all men" of Romans 5:18 with those "which receive abundance of grace and of the gift of righteousness" of verse 17. Says Shedd: "The meaning of 'all' must be determined by the context. Compare 11:32; I Cor. 15:22. The efficacy of Christ's atonement is no more extensive than faith; and faith is not universal."[13]

Other so-called universalistic passages of Scripture will be considered under the head of *Arminian Universalism.* Enough has been said to justify Charles Hodge's conclusion that the sole reason why the historic Christian church, practically as a whole, has always taught the unending punishment of the finally impenitent is that the Bible teaches it. To refer this virtual unanimity of judgment "to some philosophical speculation which has gained ascendancy in the Church," says Hodge, "would be to assign a cause altogether inadequate to the effect." He goes on to say: "Much less can this general assent be accounted for on the ground that the doctrine in question is congenial to the human mind . . . . The reverse is the case. It is a doctrine which the natural heart revolts from and struggles against, and to which it submits only under stress of authority." He adds:

10. *Zōopoieisthai.*
11. *Egeiresthai.*
12. *Commentary on Corinthians,* Edinburgh, 1887, II, 353f.
13. *Doctrinal Commentary upon the Epistle of St. Paul to the Romans.* New York, 1879, *loc. cit.*

"It is unreasonable to account for the general reception of the doctrine in question on the ground of church authority. It was universally received before the external Church arrogated to itself the right to dictate to the people of God what they must believe; and it continued to be received when, at the Reformation, the authority of the Church was repudiated, and the Scriptures were declared to be the only infallible rule of faith and practice." Hodge concludes: "The Church believes the doctrine because it must believe it or renounce faith in the Bible and give up all the hopes founded upon its promises."[14] And, speaking of the view that all men will be saved in the end, Benjamin B. Warfield remarks pointedly: "The Scriptures are too clear to the contrary to permit the indulgence of this pleasant dream."[15]

However, before unqualified universalism is dismissed it must be credited with one distinct advantage over another type of universalism. That advantage inheres in its consistency. There is a universalism which teaches that the atonement is universal in its divine design but limited in its accomplishment. Such universalism is accurately described as inconsistent. According to unrestricted universalism the atonement is as universal in its accomplishment as in its divine design. Here is no small advantage. Whatever may be said against outright universalism — and it surely lies wide open to severe criticism — it is in a position by virtue of its consistency to honor God as God by upholding such majestic declarations of His sovereignty as: "My counsel shall stand, and I will do all my pleasure " (Isa. 46:10), and "All the inhabitants of the earth are reported as nothing: and he doeth according to his will in the army of heaven and among the inhabitants of the earth; and none can stay his hand or say unto him, What doest thou?" (Dan. 4:35) Whether all thorough-going universalists actually accept the Scriptural teaching of divine sovereignty and appeal to it in

14. *Systematic Theology*, III, 870f.
15. *The Plan of Salvation*, Wm. B. Eerdmans Publishing Co., Grand Rapids, 1935, p. 94.

support of their universalism is, of course, quite another matter. The truth is that some do while others do not. Yet the fact remains that at this particular point unqualified universalism is innocent of the stupendous error of inconsistent universalism that God somehow fails to accomplish His purpose.

CHAPTER TWO

ARMINIAN UNIVERSALISM

Arminianism Prevalent in Protestantism

Widespread among so-called evangelicals or fundamentalists is the view that the atonement is universal in its divine design but limited in its actual accomplishment. God the Father and the Lord Jesus Christ, as well as the Holy Spirit, are said to have purposed the salvation of all men by the Saviour's death, and yet not all are saved in the end. For this discrepancy between the design and the accomplishment of the atonement men are accountable, for, although by virtue of the common or sufficient grace of God all are said to have the ability to believe, many refuse to receive the benefits of the atonement in faith.

That view of the design of the atonement is commonly denominated Arminian because in substance it was taught early in the seventeenth century at the University of Leyden by Jacobus Arminius. It seems not to be generally known that there are five points of Arminianism as well as five points of Calvinism. The fact is that the latter were drawn up in opposition to the former. In 1610, the year following the death of Arminius, those who shared his views drew up a so-called Remonstrance which they presented to the Dutch government. In the positive part of that document, which came to be known as "The Five Articles of Arminianism," they confessed as their belief: "That . . . Jesus Christ, the Saviour of the world, died for all men and for every man, so that he has obtained for them all, by his death on the cross, redemption and the forgiveness of sins; yet that no one actually enjoys the forgiveness of sins, except the believer, according to the word of the Gospel of John 3:16 — 'God so loved the world that he gave his only begotten Son, that whosoever believeth in him should not perish, but have everlasting life'; and in the First Epistle of John 2:2 — 'And he is the propitiation for our sins; and not for ours only, but also for the sins of the whole world.' "[1]

Arminianism has been widely held by Protestant churches and theologians and is by no means confined to such avowedly Arminian communions as the Methodist churches. Many Lutherans have welcomed Arminianism as a relief from the strict particularism of Augustinianism and Calvinism. The Latitudinarians in the Church of England at the time of the Restoration were Arminians. In the eighteenth century Arminianism was advocated by such leading writers of Great Britain as Tillotson, Jeremy Taylor, Chillingworth, Whitby, John Taylor and Samuel Clarke. It is no exaggeration to assert that Arminianism has thoroughly leavened the Christian thought of America. Even so conservative a Lutheran body as the Missouri Synod is essentially Arminian in its teaching of the design of the atonement. C. A. Beckwith is responsible for the pert and true statement: "A sign of the times is, that theological schools confessedly Arminian educate young men for Churches which are traditionally Calvinistic, and ministers holding Arminian views are received by such churches as thoroughly 'orthodox.' "[2] Evidently, Baptist William Owen Carver was under the spell of Arminianism when he concluded his article "Atonement" in *The International Standard Bible Encyclopaedia* with the undiscriminating paragraph: "Another question over which the theologians have sorely vexed themselves and each other concerns the *extent of the Atonement*, whether it is available for all men or only for certain particular, elect ones. That controversy may now be passed by. It is no longer possible to

1. Article II.
2. *The New Schaff-Herzog Encyclopedia of Religious Knowledge,* New York and London, 1908, article "Arminius."

read the Bible and suppose that God relates himself sympathetically with only a part of the race. All segregated passages of Scripture formerly employed in support of such a view have now taken their place in the progressive self-interpretation of God to men through Christ who is the propitiation for the sins of the whole world (I John 2:2). No man cometh unto the Father but by Him (John 14:6); but whosoever does thus call upon the name of the Lord shall be saved (Joel 2:32; Acts 2:21)." It is clear that the historical situation demands the serious consideration of the design of the atonement according to Arminianism.

Arminianism and the Universalistic Passages of Scripture

Those Arminians who would be known as evangelicals claim to take the Bible seriously, and the sincerity of this claim cannot be disputed. They like to refer to themselves as "Bible-believing and Bible-loving Christians," and they certainly mean to be that. To be sure, it does not necessarily follow that their understanding of Scripture is either thorough or precise, but it does follow that those passages of Scripture which they are wont to recite in support of their view must be carefully considered.

Arminianism teaches that God designed to save every individual through the atonement, but that not every individual is saved. The second part of that teaching rests squarely on Holy Scripture. At this point Arminian universalism is completely at odds with outright universalism and in perfect agreement with Calvinistic particularism. While unrestricted universalism teaches that all men are saved in the end, both Arminianism and Calvinism hold that not all will be saved. They also agree on the question who will be saved. Those will be, and only those, who believe on the Lord Jesus Christ. That this teaching is thoroughly Scriptural hardly requires proof. It is taught as unequivocally in the Bible as a whole as in the Biblical dictum: "He that believeth on the Son hath everlasting life: and he that believeth not the Son shall not see life; but the wrath of God abideth on him" (John 3:36). Both the Calvinist and the Arminian insist that only believers will enter through the gates into the city, and they so insist because the Word of God does.[3]

But what of the tenet that God designed to save every individual by the atonement? Is that also the teaching of Holy Writ? In their answer to that question Calvinism and Arminianism differ sharply. There are in Scripture a large number of passages that ascribe to the atonement a universal intent. They are commonly, and not incorrectly, called universalistic passages. Arminianism is certain that these passages teach that God designed by the death of His Son to save every single human being; Calvinism is just as positive that they teach no such thing.

In a number of places Scripture ascribes to God an unmistakably restricted design in the atonement. It is said, for instance, that Christ gave His life for His people, His sheep, His church, His elect. Such passages will be considered subsequently under the head of *Scriptural Particularism.* But already at this point in the discussion it may be remarked that in the light of such particularistic statements the great principle of Biblical hermeneutics that Scripture cannot contradict itself and is therefore its own infallible interpreter constrains the Calvinist to look for another than the Arminian interpretation of the universalistic passages. At the same time he is fully aware that his theology must be the product of unprejudiced exegesis of Holy Writ, and he is on his guard against the sinful procedure of wresting Scripture in the interest of a preconceived dogma.

Not all the universalistic passages are capable of the same

3. It hardly needs to be said that it may not be thought that this teaching leaves no room for the salvation of infants. The emphatic and sweeping statement of Jesus: "Verily, verily, I say unto thee, Except a man be born again, he cannot see the kingdom of God" (John 3:3) applies to infants as well as adults, but it is precisely in regeneration that the seed of saving faith is planted in the human heart. Regenerated infants certainly are not capable of exercising active faith, but they do possess the *habitus* of faith.

interpretation. There does not exist a single pattern of interpretation that is applicable to all of them. On the contrary, exegetically they fall into several categories.

(1) In some of the passages which teach that the atonement was for "all," for "the world," or for "every man," the meaning of these terms is restricted by the context. As in popular parlance such terms are not always intended to be taken absolutely and the context in which they occur indicates this, so also in the Bible. To use an old illustration, when Lord Nelson said: "England expects every man this day to do his duty," he evidently did not refer to every man in the world, not even to every Englishman, but only to every Englishman who was about to take part in the battle of Trafalgar. When Jesus predicted: "Ye shall be hated of all men for my name's sake" (Matt. 10:22), He surely did not mean that His disciples would be hated by every single man, woman, and child in the world, but only that worldly people, constituting the great majority of men, would hate them. When Paul said: "My manner of life from my youth . . . know all the Jews" (Acts 26:4), he cannot have meant that there was not a Jew in the world who did not know the story of his life. And when the Pharisees commented on Jesus' great popularity after the resurrection of Lazarus: "Behold, the world is gone after him" (John 11:19), they were obviously using the term "world" in a much restricted sense. A similar mode of interpretation is applicable to many of the universalistic passages. A few examples follow.

In Hebrews 2:9 it is said that God purposed that Christ "by the grace of God should taste death for every man." What is the precise meaning of the expression "every man"? In his monumental work on this epistle John Owen comments: " 'Every man' . . . is put for 'all men' by an enallage of number, the singular for the plural, for all men; that is, all those many sons which God by his death intended to bring unto glory, verse 10; those sanctified by him, whom he calls his brethren, verses 11, 12, and children given him by God, verse 13; whom by death he delivers from the fear of death, verses 14, 15; even all the seed of Abraham, verse 16."[4] F. W. Grosheide, too, holds that the meaning of "every man" is restricted by the context. Says this distinguished New Testament exegete: "The meaning of 'every man' is not that all men without distinction will reap the fruits of Jesus' death. To assume such a universalism here would contradict 'many sons,' verse 10; 'seed of Abraham,' verse 16; and 'the people,' verse 17. 'Every man' is merely the general term that is placed in the foreground and is to be defined subsequently."[5]

Another passage in which Christ is said to have died for all but in which the meaning of "all" is restricted by the context is II Corinthians 5:15, "For the love of Christ constraineth us: because we thus judge that if one died for all, then were all dead." In a sermon on this verse and the next that great New Testament scholar J. Gresham Machen asks what Paul meant by "all" and then proceeds to reply: "Well, I suppose our Christian brethren in other churches, our Christian brethren who are opposed to the Reformed Faith might be tempted to make the word 'all' mean, in this passage, 'all men' . . . . They might be tempted to interpret the words 'Christ died for all men everywhere whether Christians or not.' But if they are tempted to make it mean that, they ought to resist the temptation, since this passage is really a very dangerous passage for them to lay stress on in support of their view. In the first place, the context is dead against it . . . . All through this passage Paul is speaking not of the relation of Christ to all men, but of the relation of Christ to the Church. In the second place, the view that 'Christ died for all' means 'Christ died for all men' proves too much. The things that Paul says in this passage about those for whom Christ died do not

4. *The Works of John Owen,* Philadelphia, 1869, XII, *loc. cit.*
5. *Kommentaar op het Nieuwe Testament,* Amsterdam, 1927, XII, *loc. cit.*

fit those who merely have the gospel offered to them; they fit only those who accept the gospel for the salvation of their souls. Can it be said of all men, including those who reject the gospel or have never heard it, that they died when Christ died on the cross; can it be said of them that they no longer live unto themselves but unto Christ who died for them? Surely these things cannot be said of all men, and therefore the word 'all' does not mean all men."[6]

John 3:16 reads: "For God so loved the world that he gave his only begotten Son, that whosoever believeth in him should not perish, but have everlasting life." It may well be doubted whether there exists a more satisfying exposition of this great text than that given by Warfield in one of his sermons. He rejects every quantitative interpretation of the term "world" as it occurs here and chooses definitely for a qualitative interpretation. John 3:16 tells us that God loves the world of *sinful* humanity. Speaking of "the measure by which we are invited to measure the greatness of the love of God," Warfield says: "It is not that it is so great that it is able to extend over the whole of a big world: it is so great that it is able to prevail over the Holy God's hatred and abhorrence of sin."[7] In particular does he reject the prevalent interpretation of "world" in this verse as referring to every individual in the world. He says: "The distribution of the term 'world' in our text into 'each and every man' in the world . . . begins with the obvious misstep of directing our attention at once rather to the greatness of the world than to the greatness of God's love."[8]

(2) A great many of the universalistic passages, instead of teaching that Christ died for each and every individual, set forth the truth, which is so exceedingly prominent in the

6. *God Transcendent and Other Sermons,* edited by N. B. Stonehouse, Grand Rapids, 1949, pp. 134f.
7. *The Saviour of the World,* Hodder and Stoughton, London, New York, Toronto, 1913, p. 120.
8. *Ibid.,* p. 108.

New Testament, that salvation is for gentiles as well as Jews. For us who live in the twentieth century after Christ it is difficult, if not impossible, to grasp the novelty of that truth for the Jews of the first century of the Christian era. It impressed them as being exceedingly radical. So deeply was the fact that God showed His word unto Jacob, His statutes and His judgments unto Israel, and that He dealt thus with no other nation (Ps. 147:19f.) ingrained into the very fibre of the Jewish soul, that it rebelled violently against the notion that the middle wall of partition between Jew and gentile had been broken down and that peace was to be preached to them that were afar off as well as to them that were nigh (Eph. 2:14, 17). The Jews of that day were almost totally blind to what appears to us to be, and really is, the plain and emphatic teaching of the Old Testament: that the national church would one day blossom forth into a universal church.[9] In spite of the fact that the Master had on numerous occasions commanded the disciples to be His witnesses to the utmost parts of the earth,[10] it required a vision and a voice from heaven to convince the apostle Peter of the propriety of preaching the gospel to a Roman.[11] Small wonder that the emphasis which the New Testament places on this aspect of universalism is nothing short of tremendous.

John 12:32 affords a most interesting and clear instance of a universalistic passage of this type. Said Jesus: "I, if I be lifted up from the earth, will draw all men unto me." The next verse tells us that, in saying this, He was referring to His impending death on the cross. Did the Lord mean to say that as the crucified One He would draw to Himself in a saving way every individual in the human race? The context demands quite another interpretation. Jesus was at Jerusalem. The Passover was being celebrated. "There were

9. E.g., Gen. 12:3; Ps. 72:8-10; Ps. 86:9; Ps. 87; Dan. 2:44.
10. E.g., Matt. 28:18-20; Luke 24:46-48; Acts 1:8.
11. Acts 10.

certain Greeks among them that came up to worship at the feast" (v. 20). These Hellenes were proselytes, not Greek Jews or Hellenists, but gentiles.[12] To Philip of Bethsaida in Galilee they addressed the request: "Sir, we would see Jesus" (v. 21). Philip and Andrew conveyed this request to Jesus. Jesus was deeply moved. He envisaged the glorious salvation of the gentiles but also its prerequisite, His death on the accursed cross. He saw Himself at once as the crucified One and as the Saviour of the world. Therefore He said: "The hour is come that the Son of man should be glorified. Verily, verily, I say unto you, Except a corn of wheat fall into the ground and die, it abideth alone: but if it die, it bringeth forth much fruit . . . . Now is my soul troubled; and what shall I say? Father, save me from this hour: but for this cause came I unto this hour. Father, glorify thy name." A voice from heaven replied: "I have both glorified it, and will glorify it again" (vv. 23-28). Turning to those about Him, Jesus said: "Now is the judgment of this world: now shall the prince of this world be cast out. And I, if I be lifted up from the earth, will draw all men unto me" (vv. 31,32). In effect He declared: "My death on the cross will mark, on the one hand, the judgment of God-opposing humanity and the defeat of Satan, its prince, and, on the other hand, the supplanting of Satan's rule by My own dominion, which will extend over the whole of humanity, embracing the gentile world as well as Jewry."

In the conclusion of the well-known story of the Samaritan woman it is said that many of her people believed on Christ because of her testimony that He had told her all that ever she did; but there is added: "Many more believed because of his own words and said unto the woman, Now we believe not because of thy saying: for we have heard him ourselves, and know that this is indeed the Christ, the Saviour of the world" (John 4:42). Significantly these Samaritans denominated Jesus "the Saviour of the world." On the lips

12. See *Meyer's Commentary on the New Testament, loc. cit.*

of Samaritans, who were deeply conscious of the gulf fixed between them and the Jews, this name must have signified that they held Jesus to be the Saviour, not only of Jewry, His own nation, but of the Samaritan people as well, and by implication of all the nations of the earth. In one other place in the New Testament is Jesus called "the Saviour of the world." It, too, occurs in the writings of John. Here the apostle himself declares: "And we have seen and do testify that the Father sent the Son to be the Saviour of the world" (I John 4:14). It is much more than likely that the implications of the name in this passage are identical with its implications in the former.

John the Baptist pointed out Jesus to his disciples as "the Lamb of God which taketh away the sin of the world" (John 1:29). Whether one holds with Luther, Bengel, Olshausen and Hengstenberg that John in calling Jesus "the Lamb of God" thought of Him as the antitype of the Jewish Paschal lamb, or with Meyer that he conceived of Him as the fulfillment of such Hebrew prophecies as Isaiah 53:7, describing the Messiah as a lamb silent when led to the slaughter, or with Godet that he regarded Him in both those capacities at once, in any case it is remarkable that the Baptist asserted that this Lamb was to take away the sin of the *world.* The juxtaposition of "lamb" and "world" is striking, if indeed not surprising. In view of the fact that the Passover was an exclusively Israelitish institution and the fact that Isaiah 53 spoke of the Messiah specifically as the Saviour of "my people" (v. 8), one would have expected the Baptist to say that the Lamb of God would take away the sin of the Jewish nation. The fact is that he went much farther. He declared that this Lamb would take away the sin of the *world.* According to Meyer we have here "an extension of the earlier prophet representation of atonement for the *people,* Isaiah 53, to all *mankind.*"[13] And Calvin remarks: "When he says, the sin *of the world,* he extends this favor indiscriminately to the

13. *Ibid., loc. cit.*

whole human race, that the Jews might not think that he had been sent to them alone."[14]

Beyond all doubt, Romans 11:32, "For God hath concluded them all in unbelief, in order that he might have mercy on all," must also be interpreted as referring to both Jews and gentiles rather than to all individuals constituting the human race. The entire context points unmistakably in that direction. Nothing could be clearer than that the reference of the twofold "all" is exhausted by the two classes, Jews and gentiles, discussed in the immediate context. In the words of Warfield, "they are not to be taken individualistically but, so to speak, racially."[15]

(3) Closely related to, and sometimes hardly distinguishable from, those universalistic passsages which teach that God designed the atonement for the salvation of gentiles as well as Jews are the passages which teach that Christ by His death became the Saviour of the world as a whole, although not of everybody and everything in it, and of humanity collectively although not distributively. Scripture teaches emphatically that, while many in the world will perish, yet the world as such will be saved, and that, while not nearly every individual of the human race will be saved, those who are saved will constitute humanity. Warfield has well said: "When the Scriptures say that Christ came to save the world, that he does save the world, and that the world shall be saved by him, they do not mean that there is no human being whom he did not come to save, whom he does not save, who is not saved by him. They mean that he came to save and does save the human race; and that the human race is being led by God into a racial salvation: that in the age-long development of the race of men, it will

14. *Commentary on the Gospel according to John*, transl. by William Pringle, Edinburgh, 1847, *loc. cit.*
15. "Predestination" in *Biblical Doctrines*, Oxford University Press, New York, 1929, p. 52.

attain at last to a complete salvation, and our eyes will be greeted with the glorious spectacle of a saved world."[16]

Perhaps as striking an instance as any of this type of universalistic passage is afforded by I John 2:2: "And he is the propitiation for our sins; and not for ours only, but also for the whole world." John is writing to Christians, members of Christ's church of his day. He tells them that Christ is the propitiation for their sins. Beyond the church of that day, and for that matter of any other day before the consummation of Christ's kingdom, is the world. Does Christ's propitiatory work have any bearing on it? John says it does. He asserts that Christ is the propitiation for the whole world. No doubt, B. F. Westcott is correct in saying: "The supposition that 'for the whole world' is an elliptical expression for 'for the sins of the whole world' is not justified by usage, and weakens the force of the whole passage."[17] And Meyer is obviously right when he says: "It is incorrect to understand by 'we' the Jews, and by 'world' the Gentiles,"[18] for those to whom John was writing were by no means exclusively Jews. It is worthy of note that the apostle does not say that Christ is the propitiation for every human being in the world. He says nothing even remotely resembling that. He is not speaking of the world of men distributively. Rather, he speaks of the world in a comprehensive, a collective, a global way, and the adjective "whole" emphasizes that fact. S. Greydanus is of the opinion that the reference of "the whole world" even goes beyond the world of men. Says he: "Not all creatures and men belonging to the world have without exception propitiation for their sins in Him, but the Lord Christ has effected propitiation not merely for a part of the world, namely for that part which is constituted by the world of men, but also for the rest of the world and thus for the world in its totality, in its entire structure, in its

16. *The Plan of Salvation,* p. 131.
17. *The Epistles of St. John,* London, 1909, p. 45.
18. *Meyer's Commentary on the New Testament, loc. cit.*

fullness. The thought is the same as that of Ephesians 1:10 and Colossians 1:20."[19] Be that as it may, the very least that I John 2:2 teaches is that Christ is the propitiation for mankind collectively. The same truth was stated pointedly by the apostle Paul when he said: "God was in Christ reconciling the world unto Himself" (II Cor. 5:19). One day the whole world will be saved. In that day the church will be the world.

(4) In perusing the universalistic passages of Scripture one may never forget that certain fruits of the atonement, short of salvation, accrue to men indiscriminately and, of course, were designed by God thus to accrue. Prominent among these fruits is the so-called universal and sincere offer of salvation. A great many of the universalistic passages teach that God makes a perfectly sincere offer of eternal life to all to whom the gospel comes. To quote a few of them, Ezekiel cried: "Have I any pleasure at all that the wicked should die? saith the Lord God: and not that he should return from his ways and live?" (18:23), and again: "As I live, saith the Lord God, I have no pleasure in the death of the wicked; but that the wicked should turn from his ways and live" (33:11). Speaking of I Timothy 2:4, which says that God "will have all men to be saved and to come unto the knowledge of the truth," Machen expressed as his opinion that the teaching of this passage is identical with that of the Ezekiel passages just quoted[20] And II Peter 3:9 assures us that the Lord "is not willing that any should perish, but that all should come to repentance."

Arminians have argued that this sincere divine offer of salvation to all to whom the gospel comes presupposes the divine design to save all men through the atonement. Under

19. *Kommentaar op het Nieuwe Testament,* XIII, Amsterdam, 1929, *loc. cit.*
20. *The Christian View of Man,* The Macmillan Co., New York, 1937, pp. 74f. See also A. C. De Jong, *The Well-Meant Gospel Offer,* T. Wever Franeker, 1954, pp. 171ff.

the head *Scriptural Universalism* that argumentation will be considered more fully, but even now it may be said to find no support in Scripture. The Synod of Dort, 1618 and 1619, weighed it and found it wanting. That famous assembly of Reformed theologians, which drew up the five points of Calvinism, including the particular atonement, in opposition to Arminianism, did indeed uphold unqualifiedly the universal and sincere offer of salvation, but insisted that this offer is not a revelation of the secret counsel of God, specifically of divine predestination and of God's design in giving His Son as an atonement for sin. It is rather a revelation of God's will of complacency. This is a most pertinent distinction. "As many as are called by the gospel," say the Canons of Dort, "are unfeignedly called. For God has most earnestly and truly declared in His Word what is acceptable to Him: namely, that those who are called should come unto Him."[21] In perfect harmony with this declaration is the statement of the famous Swiss Calvinist Francis Turretin: "God delights in the conversion and eternal life of the sinner as a thing pleasing in itself and congruous with his infinitely compassionate nature."[22] The universal and sincere offer of salvation does indeed presuppose the universal love of God, which is unmistakably taught in Scripture, but it does not presuppose that God purposed the salvation of all men by the death of His Son, which is nowhere taught in Scripture.

While Scripture contains many passages which are justly denominated universalistic, there are also certain passages on which Arminians impose a universalistic interpretation. Prominent among these are the parallel passages Romans 14:15 and I Corinthians 8:11. In the context of both the apostle Paul is warning against an abuse of Christian liberty. He admonishes his readers to exercise charity toward the weaker brethren in the use of so-called indifferent things and

21. The Canons of Dort, Third and Fourth Heads of Doctrine, 8.
22. *Opera,* Edinburgh, 1867-68, IV, xvii, 33.

to give them no offense, lest some "for whom Christ died" be destroyed and perish. It has been argued that these passages imply that Christ purposed by His death to save also those who perish in the end. It is clear, however, that these passages cannot possibly be said to teach that Christ by His death designed to save *all* who perish; the very most that can possibly be claimed for them is that they teach that Christ designed to save *some* that perish. But not even that interpretation is at all plausible. Paul is warning in strong language against the offending of weak brethren. In doing that he presents, in the words of Shedd, "a supposition, for the sake of argument, of something that does not and cannot happen."[23] Another instance of this mode of argumentation is found in Galatians 1:8, where Paul envisages the impossibility of the preaching of a false gospel by an angel from heaven. Mention may also be made here of such a passage as II Peter 2:1, which warns against false teachers "denying the Lord that bought them." According to L. Berkhof, the most plausible explanation of this passage is "that given by Smeaton, as the interpretation of Piscator and the Dutch annotations, namely, 'that these false teachers are described according to their profession and the judgment of charity. They gave themselves out as redeemed men, and were so accounted in the judgment of the Church while they abode in her communion.' "[24] Hebrews 10:29, which speaks of the sure damnation of him who "hath counted the blood of the covenant, wherewith he was sanctified, an unclean thing," must be interpreted in like fashion.

Arminianism and the Scriptural System of Doctrine

Not only is the negative conclusion warranted that the universalistic passages of Scripture do not teach that God designed by the atonement to save each and every individual

23. *Dogmatic Theology,* New York, 1889, II, 481.
24. *Systematic Theology,* Wm. B. Eerdmans Publishing Co., Grand Rapids, 1946, p. 397.

or that Christ purposed by His death to save each and every individual; in the light of the system of doctrine that is taught in Holy Writ many weighty objections must be brought against the Arminian doctrine of the divine design of the atonement. It goes without saying that the Scriptural proofs for the particularistic view of the design of the atonement, several of which will be considered presently, are so many arguments against inconsistent universalism. But even at this point some serious difficulties besetting the Arminian view may be named.

Nothing is taught more emphatically in Scripture than that God is God indeed. The doctrine of the sovereignty of God lies at the very heart of Holy Writ. Isaiah declared: "Jehovah of hosts hath sworn, saying, Surely, as I have thought, so shall it come to pass; and as I have purposed, so shall it stand . . . . For Jehovah of hosts hath purposed, and who shall annul it? and his hand is stretched out, and who shall turn it back?" (Isa. 14:24, 27) No less majestic is the divine asseveration: "I am God, and there is none else; I am God, and there is none like me; declaring the end from the beginning, and from ancient times things that are not yet done; saying, My counsel shall stand, and I will do all my pleasure . . . . I have spoken, I will also bring it to pass; I have purposed, I will also do it" (Isa. 46:9-11). And the Psalmist sang: "Our God is in the heavens; he hath done whatsoever he pleased" (Ps. 115:3). To make the God of the Bible dependent on man, as does the Arminian doctrine of the design of the atonement, is to deny Him. To suppose that God is "struggling along, as it were, with the human race doing the best He can but unable to accomplish His purposes" is sacrilege. "The Arminian idea which assumes that the serious intentions of God may in some cases be defeated, and that man, who is not only a creature but a sinful creature, can exercise veto power over the plans of the Almighty God, is in striking contrast with the Biblical idea of His immeasurable greatness and exaltation by which He is removed from all the weakness of humanity."[25]

To say that the truth of the sovereignty of God lies at the heart of Scripture is identical with asserting that the doctrine of salvation by grace constitutes the very core of special revelation. Salvation by the sovereign grace of God is the central theme of Holy Writ. Salvation by grace is salvation by God. "Salvation belongeth unto the Lord" (Ps. 3:8). "It is not of him that willeth, nor of him that runneth, but of God that showeth mercy" (Rom. 9:16). "By grace are ye saved through faith; and that not of yourselves: it is the gift of God" (Eph. 2:8). Even when the regenerate co-operate with God in the process of their salvation, as they most certainly must, they do so only through the grace of God that keeps operating within them. Hence the apostolic exhortation: "Work out your own salvation with fear and trembling, for it is God which worketh[26] in you both to will and to do" (Phil. 2:12, 13). To this cardinal doctrine of the Word of God Arminian universalism does great violence, for it teaches that God did no more than make salvation possible through the death of His Son, and that it is for the sinner to make his salvation actual by the acceptance of Christ in faith of his own free volition. Thus the realization of salvation is made to depend on the will of man, not the will of God. Man becomes his own saviour. Salvation is no longer "of God that showeth mercy" but "of him that willeth."

The objection has often been brought against Arminian universalism that, if the atonement did not make the salvation of any certain, but merely rendered the salvation of all possible, the actual salvation of each individual being contingent on the free exercise of faith by him, then conceivably no one might be saved, and Christ might have died in vain. But that is far too weak a statement. The error of this type

25. Loraine Boettner, *Studies in Theology,* Wm. B. Eerdmans Publishing Co., Grand Rapids, 1947, p. 319.
26. The present participle *energōn* denotes progressing divine activity and implies the continuous dependence of the regenerate on that activity.

of universalism is much more serious. Arminianism teaches that God made the salvation of all possible by the atonement, but that it is for each man to make his salvation real by the act of accepting Christ of his own free volition as Saviour. But Scripture teaches unmistakably that apart from the grace of regeneration no man can or will exercise saving faith of his own free will. To be sure, Arminianism, prevalent Wesleyan Arminianism in particular, denies this. It tells us that every human being, unregenerate man as well as regenerate, has sufficient grace, or gracious ability, to receive Christ in faith. However, that teaching flies in the face of many plain statements of Holy Writ. Jesus, having equated coming to Him with believing on Him when He said: "He that cometh to me shall never hunger, and he that believeth on me shall never thirst," went on to affirm: "No man can come to me except the Father which hath sent me draw him" (John 6:35, 44). Lydia responded in faith to the preaching of Paul at Philippi. Significantly Scripture accounts for this fact by telling us, not that she opened her heart, but that the Lord opened her heart (Acts 16:14). Paul told the Ephesian Christians: "By grace are ye saved through faith; and that not of yourselves: it is the gift of God" (Eph. 2:8). Whether the antecedent of "it" is "faith" or the broader concept of salvation by grace through faith, in either case God is credited here with being the author of faith. The same apostle congratulated the disciples at Philippi on its having been "given" unto them "in the behalf of Christ, not only to believe on him, but also to suffer with him" (Phil. 1:29). He regarded as a gift the twofold distinction of believing on Christ and suffering with Him. According to Scripture faith is a gift of divine grace to man before it becomes an act of man. The conclusion is inescapable that, if God did no more than make salvation possible by the death of His Son and left it to man to realize his salvation by believing on Christ of his own volition, then God by the death of His Son made salvation an unrealizable possibility. And that is only another way of saying that in that case Christ not only might have died in vain, but actually must have.

Arminianism faces a dilemma. It is, of course, wholly unwilling to grant that its view of the design of the atonement involves the futility of the atonement. Yet, in order to escape that conclusion it must take its seat on one horn or the other of a most serious dilemma. Either it must teach that man is able to exercise saving faith without the regenerating grace of the Holy Spirit, or it must teach that all men actually will be saved in the end. Of the latter of these positions Berkhof has said: "It should also be noted that the doctrine that Christ died for the purpose of saving all men, logically leads to absolute universalism, that is, to the doctrine that all men are actually saved. It is impossible that they for whom Christ paid the price, whose guilt He removed, should be lost on account of that guilt. The Arminians cannot stop at their halfway station, but must go all the way."[27] As a matter of fact most Arminians take the former of these positions, but it is as patently unscriptural as is the latter. And as to the latter position, while historic Arminianism rejects it, some present-day Arminians are prepared to accept it.

Under the title *A Display of Arminianism* John Owen, sometime vice-chancellor of Oxford University, has offered what is perhaps the most conclusive refutation of Arminianism ever written. The fallacy of the Arminian view of the divine design of the atonement he set forth as follows: "God imposed his wrath due unto, and Christ underwent the pains of hell for, either all the sins of all men, or all the sins of some men, or some sins of all men. If the last, some sins of all men, then have all men some sins to answer for, and so shall no man be saved. If the second, that is it which we affirm, that Christ in their stead and room suffered for all the sins of all the elect in the world. If the first, why, then, are not

27. *Systematic Theology*, p. 395.

all freed from the punishment of all their sins? You will say, 'Because of their unbelief; they will not believe.' But this unbelief, is it a sin, or not? If not, why should they be punished for it? If it be, then Christ underwent the punishment due to it, or not. If so, then why must that hinder them more than their other sins for which he died from partaking of the fruit of his death? If he did not, then did he not die for all their sins." Having said that, Owen challenged the followers of Arminius: "Let them choose which part they will."[28]

28. *The Works of John Owen,* Edinburgh, 1862, X, 173f.

CHAPTER THREE

BARTHIAN UNIVERSALISM

A much later development in the history of doctrine than either unqualified universalism or Arminianism is what has come to be known as the dialectical theology or the new orthodoxy. Like any movement in history, it cannot be dated precisely, but it achieved prominence when, in 1919, Karl Barth published the first edition of his commentary on Paul's Epistle to the Romans.

Within the neo-orthodox camp there is nothing like unanimity as to the divine design of the atonement. Emil Brunner has found fault with Karl Barth for his brand of universalism. Reinhold Niebuhr shows, to put it mildly, definite leanings toward universalism but has expressed himself less fully on the subject than has Barth. And for Rudolf Bultmann and Paul Tillich, with their emphasis on "myths" and "symbols" in the Bible, it must become highly questionable whether Scripture teaches that there are those on whom the wrath of God will actually and literally abide forever. Nor do they manifest any great interest in that query. Existentialists that they are, they are primarily concerned about the present.

For several reasons Barth's teaching of the divine design of the atonement demands serious consideration. However he may compare with his neo-orthodox fellows as philosopher, as theologian he towers above them all. Every once in a while one hears him rated as the most influential theologian of the present generation. Although the influence exerted by a contemporary is difficult to appraise, that evaluation may well be correct. And in spite of the undeniable fact that he has departed far from the historic doctrine of the inerrancy of Scripture, it must be granted that in his theology Barth leans heavily on Scripture.

To assay Barth's doctrine of the divine design of the atonement is admittedly difficult. His radical departure, in spite of his claim to orthodoxy, from many of the positions of historic orthodoxy is a seriously complicating factor. Reference has been made to his open and even emphatic denial of the infallibility of Scripture. It is hard to believe that this denial would not inevitably cast a dark cloud over the whole of Barth's theology. The statement, occasionally made by a conservative, that his one and only objection to Barth's theology concerns the doctrine of Holy Scripture, can only be construed as shallow and undiscerning. A few examples, bearing directly on the subject at hand, must be named. Let no one think that Barth unqualifiedly accepts the orthodox teaching that Christ by His sacrificial death satisfied the divine penal justice. In his volume on Reconciliation he rejects Anselm's doctrine of the atonement. Reconciliation, says Barth, is "the conversion of man to God," and he insists that neither in Romans 5 nor in II Corinthians 5:19 does Paul speak of "an enmity of God against man which is removed by the atonement." "God," says Barth, "does not need reconciliation with men, but men need reconciliation with Him."[1] In *The Triumph of Grace in the Theology of Karl Barth*, G. C. Berkouwer gives Barth credit for his emphasis on Christ's substitution for us, but at the same time calls attention to Barth's teaching that Christ's substitution "does not mean that we do *not* come under judgment" but rather that Christ's death "*includes our dying.*" In Christ's death God is said to have smitten us with "extinction." In view of that teaching Berkouwer — with full recognition of Romans 6:1-11 — raises the serious question whether according to Barth the atonement was truly vicarious

1. *Die Kirchliche Dogmatik,* Evangelischer Verlag A. G. Zollikon, Zürich, 1953, IV, 1, 79.

in the orthodox sense of that term.[2] Also, it would be naive to suppose that whenever Barth speaks of predestination he has in mind an eternal divine decree that is certain of realization. Such is the Reformed conception of predestination, and the first article of Arminianism also speaks of it as "an eternal, unchangeable purpose" of God. But Barth employs the term more elastically. In short, by the use of orthodox terminology Barth frequently presents unorthodox thought.

The Place of Predestination in Barth's Theology

The Reformed doctrine of the particular atonement stands or falls with the Reformed doctrine of election. If God decreed from eternity to save only certain persons, it follows unavoidably that He designed by the death of His Son to save those very persons and no others. Barth's doctrine of the design of the atonement, too, is bound up inseparably with his doctrine of election. In fact, the latter of these doctrines is basic to the whole of Barth's theology. In his own words, he places election "at the beginning, even before the beginning, of all that can be said about God's dealings with His creatures"; and "The doctrine of election is the basic declaration of the gracious God as the point of departure for all divine ways and works."[3] It is clear that Barth's teaching concerning the divine design of the atonement must be approached from that angle.

So close is the relationship between Barth's doctrine of election and his doctrine of the atonement that the latter may be said to be implicit in the former. More precisely, his doctrine of the divine *design* of the atonement is not only implicit, but actually explicit in his doctrine of election. It is part and parcel thereof. Nowhere in all his *Church Dogmatics,* the volume on the Atonement or Reconciliation included, does Barth answer the question for whom Christ

2. English translation by Harry R. Boer, Wm. B. Eerdmans Publishing Co., Grand Rapids, 1956, pp. 317f.
3. *Die Kirchliche Dogmatik,* 1948, II, 2, 96, 100.

died more clearly than he does in the volume on Election. Nor need that arrangement occasion surprise. As will presently be pointed out, an integral part of Barth's doctrine of predestination is that the crucified Christ is not only the chosen man, in whom all men are elected, but also the reprobate man, bearing for all the judgment that all had merited. It follows that, according to Barth, God purposed by the death of His Son to save all men. And precisely that is his doctrine of the divine design of the atonement.

Barth versus *the Reformed Doctrine of Predestination*

At many points in his monumental and still unfinished work on dogmatics Barth claims agreement with Calvin and the historic Reformed faith as formulated in the Reformed confessions and catechisms. However, as to predestination he admittedly departs far from classical Calvinism. True, he rejects as vigorously as does any Reformed theologian the Arminian doctrine of foreseen faith as the ground of election. But he does not believe that God in His eternal counsel decreed unalterably to save only a fixed number of persons and decreed just as unalterably to allow the remainder to perish. That doctrine, he insists, does violence to the infinite love of God and fails to supply that comfort which the God of love meant His gospel to give.

Barth finds serious fault with Reformed theologians for making the double decree of predestination an expression of abstract divine sovereignty without regard to the divine love, for not stressing sufficiently the teaching of Scripture that the elect were chosen "in Christ" but, instead, reducing Christ to a mere means for the realization of sovereign election, for placing reprobation to everlasting punishment on a par with election to everlasting life as an expression of the divine good pleasure, and for teaching a doctrine of election which allows no human being to arrive at certainty concerning his election.

To brush aside those criticisms as utterly undeserved and

pointless might well be judged haughty. Nor would such procedure be completely honest. There have been exponents of the doctrine of predestination who became guilty of one or more of those errors, and not all of them were outside the Reformed fold. However, it can be shown that they were not representatives of historic Calvinism as such, and certainly not of Calvinism at its best.

Reformed theologians have ever been zealous to distinguish sharply between, on the one hand, the divine sovereignty manifest in foreordination and, on the other hand, Mohammedan fatalism and philosophical determinism. Significantly, that has come plainly to light in the controversy on predestination between Calvinists and Arminians. The latter teach that divine election is based on divine foreknowledge in the sense that God chose certain persons to eternal life because He knew from eternity that they would believe in Christ. In support of that view Arminians are wont to quote such passages as Romans 8:29, "Whom he did foreknow, he also did predestinate . . .," and I Peter 1:2, "Elect according to the foreknowledge of God the Father." On irrefutable exegetical grounds Reformed expositors insist that *knowledge* here has the pregnant meaning of *love,* which it so often has in Scripture, that *foreknowledge* is *love from eternity,* and that the teaching of these passages is that God's decree of election is rooted in His eternal love. Caspar Wistar Hodge has defined this foreknowledge as "that loving regard in God from which the Divine election springs."[4]

In distinction from Lutheran theology, Reformed theology has always held that both Christ and the church are the objects of divine election. While some Calvinists have taught that Christ was chosen as mediator in order to effect the salvation of His own and that therefore the election of men was logically prior to that of Christ, others have asserted that

4. Article "Foreknow, Foreknowledge" in *The International Standard Bible Encyclopedia,* Eerdmans, 1937. See also Geerhardus Vos, *Dogmatiek* (mimeographed), I, 1, 99, 104.

Christ was the object of election not merely as mediator but also in His capacity as head of the church and that therefore Christ's election was logically prior to that of men. Worthy of special note is what Herman Bavinck, perhaps the most scholarly and balanced of Dutch Calvinistic theologians, has said on that matter. Says Bavinck: "Christ is destined not only to be mediator but also to be the head of the church; all things were created unto Him as well as through Him. . . . Not that Christ thus became the ground and foundation of our election. But the election of the church is the very first benefit bestowed upon it; and already this benefit takes place in communion with Christ and has, not as its ground but as its end, that all other benefits, such as regeneration, faith, etc., are imparted to the church through Christ. In that sense Christ's election logically precedes ours."[5] The Second Helvetic Confession goes even farther when it affirms: "Not on account of any merit of ours, but in Christ and *on account of Christ,* God elected us."[6]

As to Barth's contention that Reformed exponents of predestination err in teaching that reprobation is willed by God in precisely the same sense as is election, a quotation from the "Conclusion" of the Canons of Dort is in order. After setting forth unequivocally, among other doctrines, that of double predestination, that is to say, the predestination of some to eternal life and of others to eternal death, the Synod of Dort, which was representative not only of the Dutch churches but of practically the entire Reformed world, thought it wise to contradict certain prevalent misrepresentations of the Reformed faith. Said that truly ecumenical Reformed council: "It clearly appears that some, whom such conduct by no means became, have violated all truth, equity and charity, in wishing to persuade the public . . . that the same doctrine teaches that God, by a mere arbitrary act of his will, without the least respect or view to any sin, has pre-

5. *Gereformeerde Dogmatiek,* Kampen, 1908, II, 424.
6. X. "Of the Predestination of God and the Election of the Saints."

destinated the greatest part of the world to eternal damnation, and has created them for this very purpose; that in the same manner in which election is the fountain and the cause of faith and good works, reprobation is the cause of unbelief and impiety." Bavinck, too, may be cited here. While insisting that the ultimate ground of both election and reprobation is the divine sovereignty,[7] he asserts: "There is a great difference between election and reprobation. All that God does, He does for His own sake. Election, too, has its cause and its end solely in God. But in the work which He brings to pass through election He rejoices. In it He sees His own virtues shining forth. The new creation is a mirror of His perfections. But that which He brings to pass in accordance with the decree of reprobation is not directly and in itself the object of His good pleasure. Sin is not itself a good. It becomes a good only because and insofar as, contrary to its nature and in spite of itself, it is compelled by divine omnipotence to contribute to the magnifying of God's honor . . . . For herein His sovereignty ultimately shines forth most brilliantly, that He can conduct evil to a good end and make it subservient to the salvation of the church, the honor of Christ and the glory of His name."[8] And that learned American Calvinist Benjamin B. Warfield, having affirmed that the elect are chosen out of "the mass of justly condemned sinners" and that "the destruction to which those that are passed by are left is the righteous recompense of their guilt," concludes: "Thus the discrimination between men in the matter of eternal destiny is distinctly set forth as taking place in the interests of mercy and for the sake of salvation."[9]

It is not true, as Barth supposes, that according to the Reformed theology election is a hidden decree in the sense that no one can be certain of his being numbered among God's chosen. Contrariwise, the Reformed doctrine of elec-

7. *Gereformeerde Dogmatiek,* II, 399.
8. *Ibid.,* II, 417.
9. "Predestination" in *Biblical Doctrines,* p. 64.

tion gives blessed assurance and inestimable comfort. Barth himself is aware of Calvin's teaching that Christ is "the mirror of election" so that through faith in Him men may make their calling and election sure.[10] The Genevan Confession of 1537 says that Christ "is presented to us as the seal of our election if we receive and embrace Him by faith." It goes on: "Since then in possessing Christ by faith we possess also life by Him, we have no need to search further into the counsel of God; for Christ is not only a mirror in which the will of God is represented to us, but also a pledge by which it is, as it were, sealed and confirmed to us."[11] The Canons of Dort, which Warfield has lauded as "a singularly well-considered, prudent, and restrained formulary,"[12] say: "The elect, in due time, though in various degrees and in different measures, attain the assurance of this their eternal and unchangeable election, not by inquisitively prying into the secret and deep things of God, but by observing in themselves, with a spiritual joy and holy pleasure, the infallible fruits of election pointed out in the Word of God," and then proceed to name as the very first of these infallible fruits "a true faith in Christ."[13]

Barth's Doctrine of Predestination and His Universalism

The question may well be asked whether Barth does justice to the historic Reformed doctrine of predestination. The answer can hardly be other than negative. However, be that as it may, Barth is thoroughly dissatisfied with that doctrine, not merely as he conceives of it, but also as it actually is. Therefore he has constructed a new and quite different doctrine of predestination. He himself speaks of "the inevitability of a total revision of the dogma."[14]

10. *Die Kirchliche Dogmatik,* II, 2, 69.
11. "Election and Reprobation."
12. "Predestination in the Reformed Confessions" in *Studies in Theology,* Oxford University Press, New York, 1932, p. 145.
13. First Head of Doctrine, 12.
14. *Die Kirchliche Dogmatik,* II, 2, 373.

As might be expected, in *Die Kirchliche Dogmatik* Barth has devoted hundreds of pages to his doctrine of election.[15] In summary it is as follows. Jesus Christ is both the subject and the object of election. He is the electing God and therefore the ground of man's election. It follows that, instead of being a dark mystery, election is historical reality. It presents a God who is not hidden but clearly revealed. Christ is not only the choosing God, He is also the chosen man. Not merely *through* Him and *with* Him but *in* Him men are elected. And predestination is double. It entails reprobation as well as election. However, let no one think that a number of men are predestined to eternal punishment, for Christ is the reprobate as well as the elect man. In His suffering and death He bore for all the penalty of sin, the divine judgment which they had deserved. Belief in the reprobation of men is a perverse belief in what God has not decreed. Reprobation becomes identified with the great exchange of Calvary, an exchange which, having been eternally decreed by God, can never be annulled. In short, predestination does indeed involve both election and reprobation, but it does not divide the human race into elect men and reprobate men. Christ is both the elect and the reprobate for all. And that, says Barth, is truly gospel. It spells "God-for-sinners."

It would seem obvious that Barth's doctrine of predestination must force him irresistibly to cast his lot with unrestricted universalism and to teach the salvation of all men. If, however, for any reason he should decline to take that position, it would seem that unavoidably he must take refuge in a qualified and inconsistent universalism which holds that because of the unbelief of some the sovereign divine decree of election falls short of complete realization. The verdict appears warranted that Barth must choose between these alternatives and that no other choice is left him. And yet, wonderful to relate, he rejects both alternatives. In other

15. II, 2, 1 – 563.

words, he refuses to face the dilemma which he himself has created by his doctrine of predestination.

If actual reprobation consists in the reprobation of Christ, not in the reprobation of sinners, it is difficult, not to say impossible, to see how the conclusion can be avoided that in the end all sinners will be saved. Frequently Barth's formulations leave no room for any other conclusion, and for that reason he has been classified as a universalist. For instance, he speaks of belief in the reprobation of men as "belief in that which God has not revealed because it is not true; belief in that which God has not decreed but has excluded in His decree."[16] Elsewhere he stresses the "impotence" of man's attempt to lead the life of a reprobate. Man is said to have merited God's destroying enmity, but that enmity was "in the election of Jesus Christ inflicted on Him, the One, and thus averted from us, the all others." God has made the life of a reprobate an "objective impossibility" for us. The unbeliever does indeed attempt to nullify the eternal divine decision, but this attempt is futile because it can never undo the fact that the divine reprobation smote Jesus Christ exclusively. The substitution on Golgotha can be denied but never undone.[17] In the volume on Reconciliation the assertion is made that Christ's death is as a matter of accomplished fact the death of all, for all died in and with Him. "His death implied, and accordingly was, our death."[18] "Reconciliation," we are told, "is indeed a comprehensive occurrence, embracing many in the One in whom it was made, and through the many embracing even all."[19] Again, it is said repeatedly that in Christ all men, Christians and heathen alike, are objectively reconciled to God, the difference between them being not "ontic" but "noetic." That is to say, as a matter of fact both alike are reconciled, but the latter do not yet know that they are reconciled. In order that they may

16. *Die Kirchliche Dogmatik*, II, 2, 184.
17. *Ibid.*, II, 2, 381f.
18. *Ibid.*, IV, 1, 325.
19. *Ibid.*, IV, 1, 276.

learn this, the gospel must be preached to them. But the "validity and scope of the atonement accomplished in Jesus Christ" are "unconditional, eternal and divine," and "the binding character of that which took place in it" is "universal, inescapable and unsurpassable."[20] In the face of such teaching the question cannot be suppressed how Barth can possibly escape unqualified universalism. One would confidently expect him to embrace it with all his mind, heart, and soul. And yet, however reluctantly, Barth teaches that perhaps not all will be saved. *Volens nolens* he has to admit that the Bible does not teach an *apokatastasis* in the sense of the ultimate salvation of every individual. Commenting on Romans 10:11, 13, "Whosoever believeth on him shall not be ashamed" and "Whosoever shall call upon the name of the Lord shall be saved," he grants that "every one who does not believe will be put to shame and every one who neglects to call will perish."[21] In his *The Triumph of Grace in the Theology of Karl Barth* Berkouwer calls attention to Barth's concession that the teaching that there are elect men and reprobate men is "a truth of the eschaton" and quotes him as saying: "Therefore we cannot say: there are elect and reprobate. We can and must believe, however, that there will be such."[22] Berkouwer also relates that, when the question was put to Barth, at the University of Debreczen, whether reprobation is not dissolved in the universal grace of God which would have all men to be saved, he replied: "We can be certain that God's lordship is and will be total in all, but what this signifies for us we must leave to God. And therefore we dare not say that in the universal grace damnation is eliminated. The Holy Scriptures speak of election and of rejection."[23]

Barth is fully aware of the responsibility of man explicit in the gospel's command to believe. Therefore he stresses

20. *Ibid.*, IV, 1, 48, 81-83, 163.
21. *Ibid.*, II, 2, 275.
22. English transl., p. 117.
23. *Ibid.*, p. 114.

the peril of eternal death to which the unbeliever exposes himself. He who persists in unbelief will perish. Here Barth is obviously on Scriptural ground. But he goes farther. In effect and by implication, although by no means admittedly, he teaches that unbelief defeats the eternal purpose of God in election. In spite of his insistence on "the impotence of unbelief," even "the impossibility of unbelief," and "the inevitability of belief," he makes statements that not only lie wide open to that interpretation but, to put it mildly, hardly allow of any other. Although the divine decree of the election of all in Christ and the reprobation of Christ for all stands firm, it may not be thought, says Barth, that the election or the reprobation of each individual was determined with finality from eternity. To say that, would amount to making God His own prisoner.[24] Rather, predestination is a continuous activity of the free God throughout time. In fact, "there is no divine election that cannot be followed by rejection and no rejection that cannot be followed by election."[25] Man may even be said to elect himself by faith and to reject himself by unbelief. His election of himself is the result of his election by God. However, his rejection of himself is in no sense a consequence of his rejection by God. The fact is that God has elected him in Christ. His sin is that he opposes God by denying his election by God. "The individual who thus opposes God is as such rejected by God. But to be such a man can only be the choice of the ungodly man himself."[26] To be sure, that there would be such individuals was included in God's plan, but only in the sense of not being willed by God.[27] "Rejected is the man who separates himself from God by opposing his election which has taken place in Christ. . . . God accepts him, but he withdraws himself from God. . . . God destines him for salvation and His service, but he chooses the joylessness of an

24. *Die Kirchliche Dogmatik,* II, 2, 202.
25. *Ibid.,* II, 2, 205.
26. *Ibid.,* II, 2, 336.
27. *Ibid.,* II 2, 499.

existence after his own caprice and to his own honor." Barth speaks of the existence of the rejected man as "the opposite" of the divine election.[28] And yet, contradictory though it may be, he is completely unwilling to grant that man's willful rejection of divine election detracts aught from the sovereignty of God as evinced in the eternal decree of election. In all of his theology he is exceedingly zealous to uphold the divine sovereignty over against human autonomy. He solemnly affirms that "God is Lord in His eternal counsel and will be in the entire realization of that counsel."[29] Unbelief is the denial that one is chosen but in no way alters the fact of one's being chosen. Synergism would place the unbeliever's decision alongside God's decision, but the truth is that the divine decision was made in opposition to the human decision and therefore cannot be annulled by any human decision.[30] The free God freely made man a free being; but human autonomy, far from destroying the theonomy, is not even its rival.[31] So reasons Barth.

It is clear that Barth confronts a dilemma. He must choose between unrestricted universalism and an inconsistent universalism reminiscent of Arminianism. It is no less clear that he refuses to adopt either of those positions. It must be noted, however, that his attitude to each of them is not the same. He rejects the former with considerable reluctance. The latter he rejects emphatically. It must further be noted that the emphatic rejection of the latter places him under a strong compulsion to accept the former, for if God willed to save all men and in fact effected salvation for all in and through Christ, and if, further, no creature can thwart that will or undo that work, it must be that all men will be saved. Therefore it is nothing strange that there are those who classify Barth as a thorough-going universalist and persist

28. *Ibid.*, II, 2, 498.
29. *Ibid.*, II, 2, 193.
30. *Ibid.*, II, 2, 213.
31. *Ibid.*, II, 2, 194ff.

in doing so in spite of his protest against being thus classified and, for that matter, against being classified at all.

Although the proverb to the effect that consistency is a jewel contains much more than a modicum of truth, it must be admitted that there may be happy inconsistencies. It need not be denied that there is such a thing as "a foolish consistency" which has aptly been described as "the hobgoblin of little minds, adored by little statesmen and philosophers and divines." Nothing is clearer than that Barth is innocent of such consistency. That he is inconsistent is undeniable. Berkouwer is by no means his severest critic. In *The Triumph of Grace in the Theology of Karl Barth* he seems determined to give Barth the full benefit of any and every doubt. Yet he is forced to the conclusion that "Barth's refusal to accept the apokatastasis cannot be harmonized with the fundamental structure of his doctrine of election."[32] Is Barth's inconsistency at this point of the happy kind? The answer to that question may well be affirmative. If all men were chosen in Christ and Christ became reprobate for all, it follows that none can perish. To say that some do perish is inconsistent. Yet that is the undeniable teaching of the Word of God, and it is admitted, albeit reluctantly, by Barth. And if, in spite of the eternal divine decree of the election of all in Christ and the reprobation of Christ in the place of all, some perish through willful unbelief, it must be that in those instances human autonomy defeats the divine purpose. To say that it does not because it cannot is inconsistent. Yet that, too, is the emphatic teaching of the infallible Word, and Barth would uphold it. Again, if man cannot defeat the divine purpose to save all men, all must be saved. To deny this is inconsistent. Yet Scripture does deny that all will be saved, and so does Barth, no matter how hesitantly. In short, by being inconsistent, rather by adding one inconsistency to another, Barth strives to avoid both the pitfall of unqualified universalism and that of a

32. English transl., p. 116.

qualified universalism which, after the manner of Arminianism, makes God dependent on man.

Happy though these inconsistencies may be, it is nonetheless evident that Barth is in serious trouble. Here, as elsewhere, the irrationalism of the dialectical theology comes clearly to light. Its characteristic "yes and no" once again prove most confusing. When a premise and a conclusion rule one another out, one or the other must be false; in fact, both may be. Barth's conclusions just noted are Scriptural and hence true. It follows as night follows day that his premise must be in error. And Barth's basic premise is his doctrine of election.

The Scriptural Doctrine of Predestination versus *Barth*

A most thorough and precise presentation of the Scriptural basis of the Reformed doctrine of predestination is found in Warfield's "Predestination," the first chapter of his *Biblical Doctrines*. He has shown that this doctrine is taught in the Old Testament as well as the New, by Jesus as well as His apostles, and most fully by the apostle Paul. He dwells at length on "three chief passages," bearing on this subject, in the Pauline epistles: Romans 8:29, 30; Romans 9, 10, 11; Ephesians 1:1-12.

In this strictly Scriptural study the author has taken pains to correct certain more or less prevalent misconstructions of the Reformed doctrine of predestination. Fatalism is ruled out by the statement: "It is not to chance, nor to necessity, nor yet to an abstract and arbitrary will, — to God acting inadvertently, inconsiderately, or by any necessity of nature, — but specifically to the almighty, all-wise, all-holy, all-righteous, faithful, loving God, to the Father of our Lord and Saviour Jesus Christ, that is ascribed the predetermination of the course of events."[33] It is denied that God decreed from eternity the damnation of certain men without reference to

33. Pp. 60f.

their sin. The affirmation is made: "It is not indeed because men are sinners that men are left unelected; election is free, and its obverse of rejection must be equally free: but it is solely because men are sinners that what they are left to is destruction"[34] and "The destruction to which those that are passed by are left is the righteous recompense of their guilt."[35] The charge is refuted that the Reformed doctrine of predestination is an abstraction with little or no practical relevance. Concerning Paul's interest in that doctrine it is asserted: "Nothing is more noticeable than his zeal in enforcing its two chief practical contents — the assurance it should bring to believers of their eternal safety in the faithful hands of God, and the ethical energy it should arouse within them to live worthily of their vocation."[36] It is observed that in the execution of His counsel of predestination God never deals with man as a mere robot but always as "an intelligent and voluntary agent."[37] Nor is election conceived of only in terms of individuals. God has indeed elected individuals to everlasting life, but those individuals, we are told, constitute the church, and their salvation will in the end constitute the salvation of the world.[38]

Beyond all doubt, Warfield excels as a reverent and balanced student of Holy Writ. He bows unreservedly before the Bible in all its parts as the very Word of God, strives zealously to regard each part in the light of the whole, and steadfastly refuses to stress any Scriptural truth to the detriment of another. It is highly significant that such a scholar finds in the Bible a doctrine of double predestination which is far different from Barth's.

The Bible teaches that before the foundation of the world God in sovereign love chose unalterably out of the fallen race of men a fixed number in Christ unto everlasting life, and

34. P. 54.
35. P. 64.
36. P. 57.
37. P. 37.
38. P. 65.

that just as sovereignly and unalterably he passed the remainder of men by and assigned them to eternal punishment for their sins. In many passages that teaching is explicit, in others it is undeniably implicit. The evidence is both unequivocal and overwhelming. Following are but a few examples. Concerning the very word employed in the New Testament to express the idea of election[39] Meyer says that it "*always* has, and must *of logical necessity* have, reference to *others,* to whom the chosen would, without the election, still belong."[40] Jesus said: "Many are called, but few are chosen" (Matt. 22:14). In His high-priestly prayer He spoke of His own, those whom the Father had given Him and He had chosen out of the world, and said that He prayed for them alone and that to them alone eternal life would be communicated (John 17:1-16). In the face of God's diverse dealings with men as evidenced in His hiding the things of the kingdom from the wise and prudent and revealing them to babes, He pronounced the theodicy: "Even so, Father: for so it seemed good in thy sight" (Matt. 11:25, 26). Luke informs us that, as a result of the preaching of Paul and Barnabas at Antioch in Pisidia, "as many as were ordained to eternal life believed" (Acts 13:48). Romans 8:29, 30 describes "the golden chain of salvation." It is taught that glorification comes only to the justified, that justification comes only to the called, that calling comes only to the elect, and that election springs from God's eternal love. Romans 9 deals with the election and rejection of Israel as a nation, and in his defense of God's rejection of the mass of contemporary Israel Paul sets forth sharply the sovereignty of God in the entire matter of salvation. By the striking examples of the sovereign acceptance of Isaac and Jacob and the sovereign rejection of Ishmael and Esau the truth is driven home that God is the potter who has "power over the clay, of the same lump to make one vessel

39. *Eklegesthai.*
40. *Meyer's Commentary on the New Testament,* on Eph. 1:4.

unto honour and another unto dishonour" (Rom. 9:21). Ephesians 1:1-12 describes in an amazing profusion of language the riches of salvation which believers have in Christ, and the strongest possible emphasis is placed on the truth that those riches are theirs only because, according to the good pleasure of the divine will, they were chosen in Christ before the foundation of the world out of the mass of sinful men unto holiness and an eternal inheritance, all to the praise of God's glory. The apostle Peter addressed his believing readers as "elect according to the foreknowledge of God" (I Peter 1:2), thus ascribing their election to the sovereign and eternal love of God; and the same apostle spoke of the stumbling of the disobedient as evidence of their appointment to unbelief, in the words: "Which stumble at the word, being disobedient: whereunto they were also appointed" (I Peter 2:8). Small wonder that Warfield said: "The Biblical writers are as far as possible from obscuring the doctrine of election because of any seemingly unpleasant corollaries that flow from it. On the contrary, they expressly draw the corollaries which have often been so designated, and make them a part of their explicit teaching. Their doctrine of election, they are free to tell us, for example, does certainly involve a corresponding *doctrine of preterition.*"[41]

Such is the Biblical doctrine of predestination. Sad to say, it has been gravely perverted in the theology of Karl Barth. In consequence, his doctrine of the divine design of the atonement is invalidated. The teaching that God purposed by the death of His Son to save all men cannot pass the test of Scripturalness. The teaching of Scripture is another.

41. "Predestination" in *Biblical Doctrines,* p. 64.

CHAPTER FOUR

SCRIPTURAL PARTICULARISM

The particularist view of the divine design of the atonement was taught by such great theologians and preachers, among others, as Augustine, Wycliffe, Luther, Calvin, Knox, Jonathan Edwards, Whitefield, Spurgeon, Charles Hodge, Archibald Alexander Hodge, Caspar Wistar Hodge, Thornwell, Kuyper, Bavinck, Warfield and Machen. It was upheld over against Arminianism by the Synod of Dort, which was constituted by representatives of most of the Reformed churches in Europe, and it is taught in all the Reformed creeds, notably in the greatest of them all, the Westminster Confession of Faith, as an essential element of that system of doctrine which is known as the Reformed faith. Today it is upheld by all consistently Reformed theologians and by those churches which are Reformed or Presbyterian not only in name but in reality.

Briefly stated, the particularist view of the divine design of the atonement is that God purposed by the atonement to save only the elect and that consequently all the elect, and they alone, are saved. Says the Westminster Confession: "As God hath appointed the elect unto glory, so hath he, by the eternal and most free purpose of his will, foreordained all the means thereunto. Wherefore they who are elected, being fallen in Adam, are redeemed by Christ, are effectually called unto faith in Christ by his Spirit working in time in due season; are justified, adopted, sanctified, and kept by his power through faith unto salvation. Neither are any other redeemed by Christ, effectually called, justified, adopted, sanctified, and saved but the elect only."[1] Again it says:

1. III, 6.

"The Lord Jesus, by his perfect obedience and sacrifice of himself, which he through the eternal Spirit once offered up unto God, hath fully satisfied the justice of his Father; and purchased not only reconciliation, but an everlasting inheritance in the kingdom of heaven, for all those whom the Father hath given unto him .... To all those for whom Christ hath purchased redemption, he doth certainly and effectually apply and communicate the same."[2] The Canons of Dort teach: "This was the sovereign counsel and most gracious will of God the Father, that the quickening and saving efficacy of the most precious death of His Son should extend to all the elect, for bestowing upon them alone the gift of justifying faith, thereby to bring them infallibly to salvation: that is, it was the will of God that Christ by the blood of the cross, whereby he confirmed the new covenant, should effectually redeem out of every people, tribe, nation and language all those, and those only, who were from eternity chosen to salvation, and given to Him by the Father; that He should confirm upon them faith, which, together with all the other saving gifts of the Holy Spirit, He purchased for them by His death; should purge them from all sin, both original and actual, whether committed before or after believing; and having faithfully preserved them even to the end, should at last bring them, free from spot and blemish, to the enjoyment of glory in his own presence forever."[3]

In this chapter that doctrine will be set forth primarily and positively in the light of the Word of God and incidentally by way of comparison with both unrestricted and inconsistent universalism. It will be argued that the glory of the Reformed doctrine of the divine design of the atonement is twofold. It does justice to all the Scriptural data bearing on the subject and, in doing that, it highly exalts the intrinsic value of the atonement. An elucidation of these claims is in order.

2. VIII, 5, 8.
3. Second Head of Doctrine, 8.

The Word of God Honors the Particular Atonement

It was already shown that the particularistic view of the design of the atonement is in harmony with the universalistic passages of Holy Scripture. It remains to be shown that this view is expressly taught by Scripture. When an angel of the Lord appeared to Joseph of Nazareth and told him not to be afraid to take Mary as his wife, that which was conceived in her being of the Holy Ghost, the angel added: "And she shall bring forth a son and thou shalt call his name Jesus: for he shall save *his people* from their sins" (Matt. 1:21). In the allegory of the good shepherd Christ foretold that He would give and lay down His life for *His sheep* (John 10:11, 15). Speaking to His disciples and referring to them He said: "Greater love hath no man than this, that he lay down his life for *his friends*" (John 15:13). Paul declared to the Ephesian elders that Christ purchased *the church* with His own blood (Acts 20:28), and he reminded all the believers at Ephesus that Christ "loved *the church* and gave himself for it" (Eph. 5:25). And when Paul wrote to the Christians at Rome that God "spared not his own Son but delivered him up for *us* all" (Rom. 8:32), he was referring, according to both the immediately preceding and the immediately following context specifically to *the elect*. All of the statements just quoted are explicit in character. In another passage Christ teaches by inescapable implication that He gave His life for none other than those whom the Father had given Him. In His high-priestly prayer He said: "I pray not for the world, but for those whom thou hast given me" (John 17:9). Indisputably Christ's sacrificial work and His intercessory work are both priestly activities and therefore simply two aspects of His atoning work. Therefore the scope of the one cannot be wider than the scope of the other. If Christ prayed exclusively for those whom the Father had given Him, He also bought only these with His blood.

Both unrestricted universalism and inconsistent universalism deny certain unequivocal teachings of Scripture. For example, the former denies the plain Scriptural teaching of the eternal punishment of the wicked, and the latter denies, whether admittedly or unadmittedly, the equally plain Scriptural teaching of the sure efficacy of the divine purposes. These views stand or fall with those denials. No such thing can be said of particularism. In order to maintain itself it does not need to deny any truth of Scripture. Positively expressed, the particularistic view of the design of the atonement fits perfectly into the system of doctrine contained in Holy Writ. Reference to a few of the outstanding teachings of Scripture will illustrate that fact.

The particularistic view of the design of the atonement does full justice to the sovereignty of God. God's purposes cannot be thwarted by man. God's plans are not contingent on the consent of man. God's counsel is sure to stand and He is certain to do all His pleasure. Therefore all those whom He designed to save by the death of His Son will be saved, not one excepted. Those whom God designed to save and those who will be saved are identical. Speaking of God's purpose to save the elect by the blood of the cross, the Canons of Dort assert: "This purpose proceeding from everlasting love toward the elect, has from the beginning of the world to this day been powerfully accomplished, and will henceforth continue to be accomplished, notwithstanding all the ineffectual opposition of the gates of hell."[4]

The particularistic view of the design of the atonement harmonizes perfectly with the Scriptural teaching of the covenant of redemption. From eternity the persons of the Holy Trinity planned the salvation of a multitude whom no man can number. An essential element in that plan was the giving by the Father to the Son of all who ultimately would be saved. Repeatedly the Saviour spoke of those whom the Father had given Him. In His high-priestly prayer He distinguished sharply between them and the world and

4. Second Head of Doctrine, 9.

clearly identified them with the heirs of eternal life. Said He: "Thine they were, and thou gavest them me . . . . I pray for them: I pray not for the world, but for them which thou hast given me, for they are thine . . . . Holy Father, keep through thine own name those whom thou hast given me, that they may be one as we are. While I was with them in the world, I kept them in thy name; those whom thou gavest me I have kept, and none of them is lost, save the son of perdition; that the scripture might be fulfilled" (John 17:6, 9, 11, 12). At this point Calvin comments: "Judas is excepted, and not without reason; for, though he was not one of the elect and of the true flock of God, yet the dignity of his office gave him the appearance of it; and, indeed, no one would have formed a different opinion of him, so long as he held that exalted office." He substantiates this comment with the fact that Judas is here called "the son of perdition." "By these words," says Calvin, "Christ means that his ruin, which took place suddenly before the eyes of men, had been known to God long before; for *the son of perdition,* according to the Hebrew idiom, denotes a man who is ruined, or devoted to destruction."[5] That Calvin's point is well taken appears from the unmistakable and most emphatic teaching of Christ elsewhere that not one of those whom the Father has given Him can possibly perish. Speaking of the sheep for whom He would give His life, the Saviour said: "And I give unto them eternal life; and they shall never perish, neither shall any man pluck them out of my hand. My Father, which gave them me, is greater than all; and no man is able to pluck them out of my Father's hand" (John 12:28, 29). Again the Saviour declared: "This is the Father's will which hath sent me, that of all which he hath given me I should lose nothing, but should raise it up again at the last day" (John 6:39). The Son as the Servant of Jehovah (Isa. 53:11) was commissioned by the Father to bear the iniquities of those whom the Father had given Him, to lay down His

5. *Commentary on the Gospel according to John, loc. cit.*

life for them, and to accomplish fully for them the work of salvation which the Father had given Him to do (John 10:18; 17:4).

The particularistic view of the design of the atonement is a necessary corollary of the Scriptural doctrine of election. If God chose out of the lost race of humanity certain persons in Christ before the foundation of the world and predestined them unto the adoption of children by Jesus Christ to Himself (Eph. 1:4, 5), it cannot but follow that God designed that those whom He had chosen in Christ would be saved by Christ. In his *Systematic Theology* Charles Hodge brings the history of Christian doctrine strongly to bear on this point. Says he: "It never was denied that Christ died specially for the elect until the doctrine of election itself was rejected. Augustine, the follower and expounder of St. Paul, taught that God out of his mere good pleasure had elected some to everlasting life, and held that Christ came into the world to suffer and die for their salvation. He purchased them with his own precious blood. The Semi-Pelagians, in denying the doctrine of election, of course denied that Christ's death had more reference to one class of men than to another. The Latin Church, so long as it held to the Augustinian doctrine of election, held also to Augustine's doctrine concerning the design and objects of Christ's death. All through the Middle Ages this was one of the distinctive doctrines of those who resisted the progress of the Semi-Pelagian party in the Western Church. At the time of the Reformation the Lutherans, so long as they held to the one doctrine held also to the other. The Reformed, in holding fast the doctrine of election, remained faithful to their denial of the doctrine that the work of Christ had equal reference to all mankind. It was not until the Remonstrants in Holland, under the teaching of Arminius, rejected the Church doctrine of original sin, of the inability of fallen man to anything spiritually good, the sovereignty of God in election and the perseverance of the saints, that the doctrine that the atonement had a special reference to the people of God was rejected. It is, therefore, a matter of history that the doctrine of election and the Augustinian doctrine as to the design of the work of Christ have been inseparably united." Hodge goes on to say: "As this connection is historical, so also is it logical. The one doctrine necessarily involves the other. If God from eternity determined to save one portion of the human race and not another, it seems to be a contradiction to say that the plan of salvation had equal reference to both portions; that the Father sent his Son to die for those whom He had predetermined not to save, as truly as, and in the same sense that He gave Him up for those whom He had chosen to make the heirs of salvation."[6]

The particularistic view of the design of the atonement is in perfect agreement with the Scriptural teaching of the special love of God. Occasionally one hears it said by Calvinists that God is good and benevolent to all the children of men but that He loves only the elect. According to Scripture, however, it may be said without the slightest hesitation that God loves all men. Did not Jesus say: "Love your enemies, bless them that curse you, do good to them that hate you, and pray for them which despitefully use you and persecute you; that ye may be the children of your Father which is in heaven . . . . Be ye therefore perfect, even as your Father which is in heaven is perfect" (Matt. 5:44, 45, 48)? But what Scripture does not teach is that God loves all men equally. On the contrary, it tells us that His love for the elect differs qualitatively from His love for others. Now it is to "that peculiar, mysterious, sovereign, immeasurable love which passes knowledge, of which his own people, the Church of the first-born whose names are written in heaven, are the objects"[7] that the gift of Christ as Redeemer is time and again referred. "Greater love hath no man," said Jesus, "than this, that a man lay

6. II. 547f.
7. *Ibid.*, II, 549.

down his life for his friends" (John 15:13). "God commendeth his love toward us," said Paul, "in that, while we were yet sinners, Christ died for us" (Rom. 5:8). Speaking specifically of the elect, the same apostle said: "He that spared not his own Son, but delivered him up for us all, how shall he not with him also freely give us all things?" And in almost the next breath he exclaimed: "Who shall separate us from the love of Christ?" (Rom. 8:32, 35) The apostle of love said: "Hereby perceive we the love of God because he laid down his life for us" (I John 3:16), and "Herein is love, not that we loved God, but that he loved us, and sent his Son to be the propitiation for our sins" (I John 4:10).

The particularistic view of the design of the atonement is an integral part of that teaching which constitutes the very heart of special revelation — salvation by grace. The five points of Calvinism are often ridiculed as expressions of the narrowest kind of dogmatism. The truth is that they are nothing else than an undiluted presentation of the precious Scriptural doctrine of salvation by grace. Nothing is taught more emphatically in Holy Writ than that salvation is by the grace of God and by it alone. And yet there is no doctrine of Scripture which the church in the course of its history has found more difficult to maintain. Always there were influential leaders in the church who in one way or another sought to compromise this doctrine, and times without number the church gave heed to their siren songs. But beyond all doubt salvation by grace is the teaching of Isaiah, of Jesus, of Paul, of Peter, of the whole of Scripture. When the early church lost sight of it, Augustine rediscovered it. When the church of the Middle Ages lost sight of it, Luther and Calvin rediscovered it. When the churches of the Reformation were sorely tempted by Arminianism to depart from it, the Synod of Dort and the Westminster Assembly again confirmed it. And when more recently several Reformed and Presbyterian churches relegated it to the limbus of outdated and outmoded dogmas, God raised up such men as the Hodges, James H. Thornwell, Benjamin B. Warfield, Abraham Kuyper, and Herman Bavinck, not merely to defend it, but to exalt it. The doctrine of salvation by grace is the heart not only of Calvinism, but of Scripture and of Christianity. With it Christianity stands or falls. Every departure from it, no matter how small, is a departure from Christianity. Next to the Bible itself the clearest and purest expression of this doctrine is found in the five points of Calvinism. And they are just so many links of a chain, dependent on one another and supporting one another. God in His sovereign good pleasure from eternity elected certain persons in Christ to everlasting life. By nature the elect, like all other men, are totally depraved sinners who cannot save themselves. In order to save the elect God sent His Son into the world to purchase redemption for them by His precious blood and perfect obedience. By the atonement Christ merited for the elect the Holy Spirit, who effectually regenerates them and works the gift of saving faith in their hearts. That God's chosen, whom Christ has redeemed and to whom the Holy Spirit has applied redemption, should perish is entirely out of the question. Those are the five points of Calvinism. Together they constitute one doctrine — that of salvation by sovereign grace.

The Particular Atonement Exalts the Saving Work of Christ

The glory of the particularistic doctrine of the divine design of the atonement lies in its consistently Scriptural character. Small wonder that its glory also lies in its exaltation of the value of the atonement. For the value which Scripture ascribes to the atonement is high indeed.

Inconsistent universalism, like unrestricted universalism, seeks to convey the impression that it exalts the atonement far more than does Calvinism. It boasts of having an atonement for all while Calvinism is said to have an atonement for some only. It glories in a universal, a limitless, atonement in contrast with the limited atonement of the Reformed faith. But such boasting and glorying are vain.

The notion is prevalent that, while according to inconsistent universalism a great many will be saved, according to Calvinism few will enter through the gates into the eternal city. But that notion is absurd. According to both Calvinism and inconsistent universalism, whether represented by Barth or by Arminianism, all who believe on the Lord Jesus Christ will be saved and no others. On this point there is no difference. No less absurd is the charge, sometimes brought against Calvinism, that it teaches by implication, if not explicitly, that a truly repentant sinner may fail of salvation because he does not happen to be numbered among the elect, whose redemption Christ purchased on Calvary. It goes altogether without saying that all the elect, and only the elect, will truly repent of their sins and seek salvation in Christ, for repentance is a fruit of election as well as a benefit of the atonement. And it is the unqualified teaching of Calvinism that genuine repentance never comes too late. The Saviour's assurance, "Him that cometh to me I will in no wise cast out" (John 6:37) is a favorite text with Calvinistic preachers. The Calvinist rejoices in the Biblical attestation that, when all the elect shall have been gathered in, they will constitute a throng which no man can number and which will be as countless as the grains of sand on the seashore and as the stars that sparkle in the black-blue firmament of night. Says Shedd in his *Dogmatic Theology*: "In saying that Christ's atonement is limited in its application . . . it is meant that the number of persons to whom it is effectually applied is a fixed and definite number. The notion of definiteness, not of smallness, is intended . . . . The circle of election and redemption must indeed be a circumference, but not necessarily a small one. No man is redeemed outside of the circle. All the sheep must be within the fold. But the circle is that of the heavens, not of the earth."[8]

In his sermon, already referred to, on II Corinthians 5: 14, 15, Machen calls attention in his own inimitably tender way to the comforting character of the Reformed doctrine of the design of the atonement and contrasts it with the gloominess of the teaching of Arminianism on the same subject. He begins: "People say that Calvinism is a dour, hard creed. How broad and comforting, they say, is the doctrine of a universal atonement, the doctrine that Christ died equally for all men there upon the cross! How narrow and harsh, they say, is this Calvinistic doctrine — one of the 'five points' of Calvinism — this doctrine of the 'limited atonement,' this doctrine that Christ died for the elect of God in a sense in which He did not die for the unsaved!" He continues: "But do you know, my friends, it is surprising that men say that. It is surprising that they regard the doctrine of a universal atonement as being a comforting doctrine. In reality it is a very gloomy doctrine indeed . . . . Ah, if it were only a doctrine of a universal salvation, instead of a doctrine of a universal atonement, then it would no doubt be a very comforting doctrine; then no doubt it would conform wonderfully well to what we in our puny wisdom might have thought the course of the world should have been. But a universal atonement without a universal salvation is a cold, gloomy doctrine indeed. To say that Christ died for all men alike and that then not all men are saved, to say that Christ died for humanity simply in the mass, and that the choice of those who out of that mass are saved depends upon the greater receptivity of some as compared with others — that is a doctrine that takes from the gospel much of its sweetness and much of its joy. From the cold universalism of that Arminian creed we turn ever again with a new thankfulness to the warm and tender individualism of our Reformed Faith, which we believe to be in accord

8. II, 474.

with God's holy Word. Thank God we can say every one, as we contemplate Christ upon the Cross, not just: 'He died for the mass of humanity, and how glad I am that I am amid that mass,' but: 'He loved me and gave Himself for me; my name was written from all eternity upon His heart, and when He hung and suffered there on the Cross He thought of me, even me, as one for whom in His grace He was willing to die.' "[9]

Calvinism does indeed hold that the number of those whom God designed to save by the death of His Son is limited, but it does not limit the intrinsic value of the atonement. This is a fact of the greatest moment. Inconsistent universalism seriously restricts the efficacy of the atonement. Arminianism teaches that the atonement does no more than make salvation possible; and, as was already pointed out, by unashamedly making the realization of salvation contingent on the will of man, it teaches in effect that the atonement makes salvation an unrealizable possibility. Calvinism, on the contrary, insists that the atonement actually saves all whom it was intended to save. Their doctrine of the divine design of the atonement being what it is, neither the Arminian nor Barth can take that position without concluding that all men will be saved. Therefore the evangelical Arminian rejects that position without hesitation. And Barth, leaning heavily toward unqualified universalism and yet not ready to embrace it, cannot accept that position. The conclusion is inescapable that of the three only the Calvinist teaches a truly effective atonement.

What does Calvinism mean when it insists that the atonement actually saves? By His passive obedience, that is to say, by His obedience manifest in His suffering,[10] particularly in His death on the cross, Christ fully atoned for the sins

9. *God Transcendent and Other Sermons,* p. 136.

10. When theologians describe Christ's obedience manifest in His suffering as "passive," they have in mind the Latin *pati,* to suffer, and do not mean to convey the thought that in His suffering Christ was merely acted upon and was not active. He was active in His very death, for He "laid down His life" (I John 3:16).

of the elect; consequently there is no condemnation for them, nor will there be in the future. Not only that, but by His active obedience, His life in perfect harmony with the law of God, He merited for the elect the positive benefit of eternal life. Thus by His passive and active obedience, which are inseparable and together may be said to constitute the atonement, Christ wrought full salvation for the elect. It must not be thought, however, that the elect are saved automatically. In bringing them to salvation God deals with them, not as so many things, but as rational and moral beings; that is, as free agents. Therefore He requires of them faith in the Lord Jesus Christ. However, the atonement guarantees that they will receive the gift of faith. Such ethical benefits of salvation as regeneration and faith are fruits of the atonement as well as is the forensic benefit of justification. In other words, by the atonement Christ merited for the elect the Holy Spirit, who imparts to them the new birth and saving faith. Still further, also the ethical benefits of sanctification and perseverance are guaranteed by the atonement and flow directly from it as their fountain-head. The same is true of ultimate glorification. All that is implied in the Pauline asseveration: "Whom he did predestinate, them he also called; and whom he called, them he also justified; and whom he justified, them he also glorified . . . . He that spared not his own Son, but delivered him up for us all, how shall he not with him also freely give us all things?" (Rom. 8:30, 32). The expression "all things" does not embrace everything in the universe but, in harmony with the context, "the whole of what He has to bestow in accordance with the aim of the surrender of Jesus, . . . the collective saving blessings of His love shown to us in Christ."[11] In brief, the atonement not only renders the salvation of all the elect completely certain, but the realization of their salvation in all its parts was *procured* by the atonement. Says the Westminster Larger

11. *Meyer's Commentary on the New Testament, loc. cit.*

Catechism: "Christ, by his mediation, hath procured redemption, with all other benefits of the covenant of grace."[12]

Commenting on the statement by Arminian Henry C. Sheldon of Boston University: "Our contention is for the universality of the opportunity of salvation, as against an exclusive and unconditional choice of individuals to eternal life,"[13] Warfield remarks: "There is to be noted in this declaration, 1) the conscious stress on universalism as the characteristic note of Wesleyanism and 2) the consequent recognition that all that God does looking toward salvation is to afford an opportunity of salvation; so that what is actually contended for is not that God does not save some only but that he really saves none, — he only opens a way of salvation to all and if any are saved they must save themselves. So inevitable is it that, if we assert that all that God does looking to salvation he does to and for all alike and yet that not all are saved, we make all that he does fall short of actual salvation: no one must receive more than he who receives the least."[14] In sharp contrast with that view of the design of the atonement stands the Reformed view that God by the atonement designed to save and actually does save all who ultimately are saved.

In reference to the popular notion that all men are entitled to "an equal chance" at salvation, Warfield says: "Shall we not fix it once for all in our minds that salvation is the right of no man; that a 'chance' to save himself is no 'chance' of salvation for any; and that, if any of the sinful race of man is saved, it must be by a miracle of almighty grace, on which he has no claim, and, contemplating which as a fact, he can only be filled with wondering adoration of the marvels of the inexplicable love of God?"[15] That miracle of almighty grace is the atonement.

The same scholarly divine draws the line of demarcation

12. Question 57.
13. *System of Christian Doctrine,* 1903, p. 417.
14. *The Plan of Salvation,* p. 99.
15. *Ibid.,* pp. 101f.

between Calvinism and Arminianism sharply when he asserts: "The issue is indeed a fundamental one and it is closely drawn. Is it God the Lord that saves us, or is it we ourselves? And does God the Lord save us, or does he merely open the way of salvation, and leave it, according to our choice, to walk in it or not? The parting of the ways is the old parting of the ways between Christianity and autosoterism. Certainly only he can claim to be evangelical who with full consciousness rests entirely and directly on God and on God alone for his salvation."[16] According to the particularistic view of the design of the atonement, the atonement not merely makes salvation possible but actual; and that is another way of saying that the sinner is not saved by himself but by God, and by God alone. That is Calvinism not only, but that is of the very essence of Christianity. Arminian universalism is a departure, and a serious one, from Christianity. Particularism is consistent Christianity.

In the foregoing paragraphs the particular design of the atonement was contrasted primarily with Arminian universalism. There was good reason for so doing, for historically the Reformed doctrine of the design of the atonement acquired its most precise formulation in the crucible of the Arminian controversy in Holland. Not everything that was said is applicable to Barthian universalism. For instance, the charge of "autosoterism" does not apply to Barthianism as it does to Arminianism. According to Arminianism saving faith is not a gift of God but an act of the free will of man of which even the unregenerate is capable. That makes man his own saviour. According to Barth faith is indeed a human act but, prior to that, a gift sovereignly bestowed by the Holy Spirit.[17] Salvation, then, belongs to the Lord. At this precise point Barth subscribes to the Biblical doctrine of salvation by grace, and that, no doubt, is

16. *Ibid.,* p. 108.
17. *Die Kirchliche Dogmatik,* IV, I, 826ff.

one reason for his speaking repeatedly of "the triumph of grace" in his theology. Yet the fact remains that Barthianism, like Arminianism, does violence to the sovereign love and the loving sovereignty of God manifest in the atonement, by withholding assent to the proposition that the atonement saves all without exception whom God purposed to save by it. That, too, is a significant departure from the Reformed faith and, it must be said, from Christianity.

Nor may it be forgotten that in important respects Barth departs much farther from the Scriptural doctrine of the atonement than does evangelical Arminianism. Beyond all doubt, evangelical Arminianism teaches a vicarious atonement; whether the atonement according to Barth is vicarious in the historic sense of that term is, as was already pointed out, highly questionable. Evangelical Arminianism teaches that Christ's sacrifice on the cross appeased the wrath of God against sin; Barth holds, as does theological liberalism, that God did not need to be, and was not, reconciled to sinners by the death of His Son, but they were reconciled to God. Evangelical Arminianism is completely certain that not all men will be saved and therefore it definitely rejects unqualified universalism; Barth has strong leanings toward unqualified universalism and admits with reluctance that some will be lost. And Barth's rejection of the Arminian error of foreseen faith as the ground of election does not prove that he holds a higher view of election than does Arminianism. In a most important respect his view is lower. For, although according to both Barth and Arminianism not all will be saved whom God designed to save by the death of His Son, yet Arminianism insists that all whom God *predestined* to eternal life will be saved, and to that position Barth does not hold consistently. In other words, historic Arminianism teaches an election which is not universal but unalterable; Barth teaches an election which is universal but not unalterable. Here Arminianism is on Scriptural ground, Barth is not.

CHAPTER FIVE

SCRIPTURAL UNIVERSALISM

It is rather commonly supposed that what was said in the foregoing chapter constitutes the sum total of the Reformed doctrine of the divine design of the atonement. That is by no means the case. According to the Reformed faith the divine design of the atonement is indeed in an important respect limited. But the Reformed faith also insists that in other important respects it is universal. It can be shown without the slightest difficulty that certain benefits of the atonement, other than the salvation of individuals, are universal. That being the case, it follows of necessity that God designed that this should be so. It is the sheerest folly to say that, while God designed to save the elect through the death of His Son, all other results of the atonement are accidental and lie without the pale of the divine purpose. God purposed everything that comes to pass, all the fruits of the atonement included. Therefore the statement, so often heard from Reformed pulpits, that Christ died only for the elect must be rated a careless one. To be sure, if by "for" be meant *in the place of,* the statement is accurate enough, for those in whose stead Christ suffered the penalty of sin will not themselves have to suffer that penalty, and therefore their salvation from that penalty is assured. If, however, by "for" be meant *in behalf of,* it is inaccurate, to say the least. Certain benefits of the atonement accrue to men generally, including the non-elect. Like all things that are, this is so by divine design. Charles Hodge is right when he says: "There is a sense, therefore, in which He died for all, and there is a sense in which He died for the elect only."[1]

Let it be understood that the Calvinist has no monopoly on the Scriptural teaching of the universal design of the atonement. He does not stand alone in upholding those universal aspects of the atonement that are to be considered presently. For example, to assert that the Arminian has no interest in the proclamation of a free offer of the gospel, that Barth questions the sufficiency of the atonement for all, or that the thorough-going universalist overlooks the truth that the world will in the end be saved, would so obviously be to fly in the face of facts as to deserve to be branded preposterous. Nevertheless, it can be shown that the Calvinist, and he alone, precisely because of his particularism is in a position to do full justice to Scriptural universalism. The particular design of the atonement and its universal design in no way contradict each other. Nor do they merely complement each other. They support and strengthen each other. In final analysis they stand and fall together. The Calvinist can be, must be, and, inconsistencies aside, will be an ardent universalist because he is a zealous particularist.

The Universal Suitableness and Sufficiency of the Atonement

Says Charles Hodge: "What was suitable for one was suitable for all. The righteousness of Christ, the merit of his obedience and death, is needed for justification by each individual of our race, and therefore is needed by all. It is no more appropriate to one man than to another. Christ fulfilled the condition of the covenant under which all men were placed. He rendered the obedience required of all, and suffered the penalty which all had incurred; and therefore his work is equally suited to all."[2]

The same divine, speaking of Christ's satisfaction, says: "Its value depends on the dignity of the sacrifice; and as no

1. *Systematic Theology*, II, 546.
2. *Ibid.*, II, 545.

limit can be placed to the dignity of the Eternal Son of God who offered himself for our sins, so no limit can be assigned to the meritorious value of his work. It is a gross misrepresentation of the Augustinian doctrine to say that it teaches that Christ suffered so much for so many; that He would have suffered more had more been included in the purpose of salvation. This is not the doctrine of any Church on earth, and never has been. What was sufficient for one was sufficient for all. Nothing less than the light and heat of the sun is sufficient for any one plant or animal. But what is absolutely necessary for each is abundantly sufficient for the infinite number and variety of plants and animals which fill the earth. All that Christ did and suffered would have been necessary had only one human soul been the object of redemption; and nothing different and nothing more would have been required had every child of Adam been saved by his blood."[3]

The Canons of Dort declare: "The death of the Son of God is the only and most perfect sacrifice and satisfaction for sin, and is of infinite worth and value, abundantly sufficient to expiate the sins of the whole world," and "Whereas many who are called by the gospel do not repent nor believe in Christ but perish in unbelief; this is not owing to any defect or insufficiency in the sacrifice offered by Christ upon the cross, but is wholly to be imputed to themselves."[4]

If the atonement was suitable for all and sufficient for all, it goes wihout saying that God designed that it should be such. Therefore Owen says: "It was the purpose and intention of God that his Son should offer a sacrifice of infinite worth, value and dignity, sufficient in itself for the redeeming of all and every man."[5] And Berkhof says discerningly, although not altogether lucidly: "The Schoolmen were accustomed to saying that Christ died sufficiently for all men, but

3. *Ibid.,* II, 544f.
4. Second Head of Doctrine, 3 and 6.
5. *The Death of Death in the Death of Christ,* Philadelphia, 1865, IV, I, I.

efficaciously for the elect.[6] This language was adopted by some orthodox theologians and even by Calvin. But after the extent of the atonement had been made the object of special study, Reformed theologians generally refused to state the truth in that form, because it was apt to give the impression that Christ in dying intended that all men should share in the proper effects of His atoning death. They prefer to say that the death of Christ viewed objectively and apart from His design and purpose, was inherently sufficient for all, though efficacious only for the elect."[7] It hardly needs to be noted that Berkhof cannot mean to say that God did not design that the atonement should be objectively sufficient for all. God most assuredly designed that, for He purposed all that is.

Common Grace

The Reformed doctrine of common grace is not as yet a finished product. Rather, it is in process of development, witness Cornelius Van Til's contribution in a number of articles on that theme, which were first published in *The Westminster Theological Journal* and subsequently appeared as a book,[8] and James Daane's evaluation of Van Til's doctrine of common grace in *A Theology of Grace.*[9] It may, however, be asserted without hesitation that God in His longsuffering does not yet see fit to pour out upon the reprobate the full content of the vials of His righteous judgment, but is "the Saviour," that is, the Preserver, "of all men" (I Tim. 4:10); that for the present He takes an attitude of benevolence, which Scripture does not hesitate to denominate "love," toward all men, including His enemies, in virtue of which He dispenses certain blessings to them as, for instance, rain

6. *Sufficienter pro omnibus, sed efficaciter tantum pro electis.*
7. *Vicarious Atonement through Christ,* Wm. B. Eerdmans Publishing Co., Grand Rapids, 1936, p. 176.
8. *Common Grace,* The Presbyterian and Reformed Publishing Co., Philadelphia, 1947.
9. Wm. B. Eerdmans Publishing Co., Grand Rapids, 1954.

and sunshine (Matt. 5:43-48); that He restrains sin in the reprobate, as a result of which more or less orderly human society remains possible (Gen. 6:3; 20:6); and that He endows the unregenerate not only with natural talents in such fields as science and art (Gen. 4:20-22), but also with certain virtues which enable them to do so-called civic good (Luke 6:33), although not such good as is prompted by faith in God and love for Him and is known as spiritual good. The question whether this goodness of God to men in general is properly called "grace" or should be denominated otherwise is relatively unimportant if only it be maintained, as Reformed theologians have consistently done, that the difference between saving grace and common grace is not quantitative but qualitative. No amount of common grace equals so much as a grain of saving grace.

What has been said is admittedly an incomplete statement of the doctrine of common grace, and the theme under discussion does not require a fuller statement. What the theme does demand is a consideration of the question whether or not the blessings of the common grace of God are a product of the atonement.

One can hardly escape the impression that a number of Reformed theologians have fought shy of that question. It has difficult aspects. However, Scripture teaches repeatedly that God shows mercy to the wicked because of the righteous. In answer to Abraham's intercessory prayer God assured him that He would spare Sodom for the sake of but ten righteous men that might conceivably be found within it (Gen. 18:32); and a plain implication of Jesus' words addressed to His disciples, "Ye are the salt of the earth" (Matt. 5:13), is that because of the presence of His people, acting as a preservative, God has not yet spewed this insipid and putrid world out of His mouth. This teaching of Scripture points plainly to some connection between the atonement and the common grace of God. In *Calvin on Common Grace* Herman Kuiper says guardedly that Calvin "does create the impression that he believed that the non-elect enjoy within the limits of this present life certain fruits of the mediatorial labors of Christ by which He acquired heaven and earth as the inheritance of God's children." He proceeds: "Calvin does not say this in just so many words but he does suggest the thought that Christ, into whose hands the Father has delivered all things, so dispenses temporal gifts that the ungodly receive the crumbs which fall from the table which He has prepared for those whose sins He bore on the cross."[10] Berkhof tells us: "Reformed theologians generally hesitate to say that Christ by His atoning blood merited these blessings for the impenitent and reprobate. At the same time they do believe that important natural benefits accrue to the whole human race from the death of Christ, and that in these benefits the unbelieving, the impenitent, and the reprobate also share."[11] In support of this observation he quotes William Cunningham to the effect that "many blessings flow to mankind at large from the death of Christ, collaterally and incidentally, in consequence of the relation in which men, viewed collectively, stand to each other."[12] He further cites Robert S. Candlish to the effect that "the entire history of the human race, from the apostasy to the final judgment, is a dispensation of forbearance in respect to the reprobate, in which many blessings, physical and moral, affecting their characters and destinies forever, accrue even to the heathen, and many more to the educated and refined citizens of Christian communities. These come to them through the mediation of Christ, and coming to them now, must have been designed for them from the beginning."[13]

The final sentence of the quotation from Candlish is particularly significant for the present discussion. The blessings of common grace, although resulting only indi-

10. *Calvin on Common Grace,* Oosterbaan and Le Cointre, Goes, 1928, p. 214.
11. *Systematic Theology,* p. 438.
12. *Historical Theology,* Edinburgh, 1871, II, 333.
13. *The Atonement,* London, 1861, pp. 358f.

rectly from the atonement, were most surely designed by God to result from the atonement. The design of God in the atoning work of Christ pertained primarily and directly to the redemption of the elect, but indirectly and secondarily it also included the blessings of common grace. Berkhof's statement that "all that the natural man receives other than curse and death is an indirect result of the redemptive work of Christ"[14] is not too sweeping. God planned it thus.

The Universal and Sincere Offer of Salvation

No other blessing of the common grace of God is as great as is the universal and sincere offer of salvation, nor is any other more obviously a fruit of the atonement. Therefore it deserves separate treatment.

When Reformed theologians speak of the gospel offer of salvation as universal, they do not mean what certain Lutheran theologians have meant by the same term. Old Lutheranism, alleging that the honor of God requires that, looking to salvation, He shall make the same provision for all men, taught that Christ died to take away the sin of the whole world and that the proclamation of this good news actually reaches all men without exception. More specifically it was said that in three periods of history, the time of Adam, the time of Noah and the time of the apostles, the gospel was made known to all men then living, and that indirectly, by tradition, if not directly, it came also to all their descendants. But this contention was so obviously contrary to plain fact that after a while Lutheran theology ceased to make it in that form. According to the Norwegian divine Lars Nielsen Dahle, more recent conservative Lutheran theologians say that "the universality of the call is a necessary presupposition, a postulate, which must be assumed on the ground of the testimony of Scripture regarding God's universal saving-will on the one hand, and of the Scripturally established truth

14. *Systematic Theology*, p. 439.

on the other that this saving-will cannot be realized for the individual unless God's call actually reaches him; but how this happens we cannot say, for it is a fact that at the present day it has only reached comparatively few, or at most a minority of mankind."[15]

The Reformed view of the universality of the gospel call is quite another. God has commanded His church to preach the gospel to all men everywhere. Yet there have been in every age a great many who never heard the glad tidings of salvation. Before the end of time the good news will have reached every kindred and people and nation. But at no time is the gospel confined to any nation or, for that matter, to any particular class of men. It is intended for Jews, Greeks, barbarians and Scythians (Col. 3:11). It comes to both the regenerate and the unregenerate, the elect and the non-elect. To say that such invitations as: "Ho, every one that thirsteth, come ye to the waters, and he that hath no money; come ye, buy and eat; yea come, buy wine and milk without money and without price" (Isa. 55:1), and "Come unto me, all ye that labor and are heavy laden and I will give you rest" (Matt. 11:28) are intended only for those who, having been born again through the grace of the Holy Spirit, have come to realize their lost condition, is to limit the meaning of Scripture without warrant. Let it be said emphatically that the Reformed theology does not teach, as some allege, that the gospel invitation is only for the elect and the regenerate. That allegation is nothing but a caricature of Calvinism. Ezekiel 3:19 is one of many Scripture passages which teach that the invitation comes also to the non-elect and the unregenerate. Here God says to the prophet: "If thou warn the wicked, and he turn not from his wickedness, nor from his wicked way, he shall die in his iniquity; but thou hast delivered thy soul." The same truth is taught indubitably in the plaintive words of the weeping Lord Jesus recorded in Matthew 23:37, "O Jerusalem, Jerusalem, thou

15. *Life after Death,* pp. 184f.

that killest the prophets and stonest them which are sent unto thee, how often would I have gathered thy children together even as a hen gathereth her chickens under her wings, and ye would not." The Canons of Dort, speaking of "the promise of the gospel that whosoever believes in Christ crucified shall not perish but have eternal life," declare: "This promise, together with the command to repent and believe, ought to be declared and published to all nations, and to all persons promiscuously and without distinction, to whom God out of His good pleasure sends the gospel."[16]

When the Reformed theology describes the universal offer of salvation as sincere, it does not merely mean that the human preacher, who obviously cannot distinguish with certainty between the elect and the non-elect, must for that reason issue to all men indiscriminately a most sincere offer of eternal life and an equally sincere invitation to accept that offer. It most assuredly means that, but it means incomparably more. The Reformed theology insists that God Himself, who has determined from eternity who are to be saved and who are not, and therefore distinguishes infallibly between the elect whom He designed to save by the death of Christ and the reprobate whom He did not design to save, makes on the ground of the universally suitable and sufficient atonement a most sincere, *bona fide,* offer of eternal life, not only to the elect but to all men, urgently invites them to life everlasting, and expresses the ardent desire that every person to whom this offer and this invitation come accept the offer and comply with the invitation.

It cannot be denied that the Calvinist here faces a paradox. Significantly, he has no interest in denying the paradox, if only the term *paradox* be given its proper content. Not for a moment does he subscribe to the implied tenet of the dialectical theology that truth is irrational. He does not admit that the Reformed doctrine of the particular design of the

16. Second Head of Doctrine, 5.

atonement and the Reformed doctrine of the universal and sincere offer of salvation actually contradict each other, but he readily grants that there is a *seeming* contradiction here which he is unable to reason away. Like the truths of divine sovereignty and human responsibility, he regards also these two truths as parallel Scriptural lines which, so far as human eye can see and human reason can understand, never meet, but which do actually meet in the infinite God. He subjects human logic to the divine *logos.* Realizing that human reason is inherently finite and, after the fall, extremely fallible, he subjects it to the infallible Word of God. And finding there, as he does, both the doctrine of the particular design of the atonement and the doctrine of the universal and sincere offer of the gospel taught with unmistakable clarity, he bows his head in humble adoration and, exclaiming: "O the depth of the riches both of the wisdom and knowledge of God, how unsearchable are his judgments and his ways past finding out! For who hath known the mind of the Lord? or who hath been his counsellor?" (Rom. 11:33), he accepts both.

Attempts have occasionally been made to make this paradox seem less paradoxical. It has been said, for instance, that God makes the sincere offer of salvation to the reprobate, not *qua* reprobate, that is, not in the capacity of reprobate, but rather in that of sinners in need of salvation. Whatever one may think of that formulation, one must insist that it does not solve the problem. Obviously God, who always sees all truth comprehensively, never abstracts the fact that a given individual is a reprobate from the fact that he is a sinner, in such a way that He is aware only of the latter. Nor is the difficulty reduced at all by the suggestion that those passages of Scripture which teach the universal and sincere offer of salvation bear on the practical matter of preaching rather than the science of theology, for that proposal involves a patently false antithesis. In his study on *Common Grace* Van Til makes the point that God deals with man on the plane of history. The complete salvation of the elect is a foregone conclusion, but they have not yet attained it. Therefore God can in a real sense be angry with them. On the other hand, the damnation of the reprobate is also a foregone conclusion, but it has not yet been consummated. Therefore God can in a real sense manifest favor to them. This has a bearing on the universal and sincere offer of salvation. "We may think," says Van Til, "of the universal offer of salvation as an evidence of common grace. It is evidence of *earlier* rather than of *lower* grace. All common grace is earlier grace. Its commonness lies in its earliness."[17] That thought has real value, but Van Til would likely be the last to claim that he has thus solved the paradox of the particular divine design of the atonement and the divinely made universal and sincere offer of salvation on the ground of the atonement. In fact, in the same study Van Til affirms that such a paradox as this one, instead of constituting a difficulty within the Reformed faith, is of its very essence. Says Van Til: "Our position is naturally charged with being self-contradictory. It might seem at first glance as though we were willing, with the dialectical theologians, to accept the really contradictory. Yet such is not the case. In fact we hold that our position is the only position that saves one from the necessity of ultimately accepting the really contradictory. We agree that unless we may hold to the presupposition of the self-contained ontological trinity, human rationality is itself a mirage. But to hold to this position requires us to say that, while we shun as poison the idea of the really contradictory, we embrace with passion the idea of the *apparently* contradictory. It is through the latter alone that we can reject the former . . . . God dwells in light that no man can approach unto. This holds of His rationality as well as of His being . . . . It follows that in everything with which we deal we are, in the last analysis, dealing with

17. P. 82.

the infinite God, this God who hideth Himself, this mysterious God . . . . To seek to present the Christian position as rationally explicable in the sense of being comprehensible to the mind of man is to defeat our own purposes. To do so we must adopt the standard of reasoning of our opponent, and when we have accepted the standard of reasoning of our opponent, we must rest content with the idea of a finite God."[18] A. C. De Jong correctly speaks of "various predications which seem to us to be contradictory, although in reality these predications are not contradictory," and asserts: "God's actions and *attitudes,* being unique, always elude exhaustive logical analysis."[19]

There is a decided strain of rationalism in Arminianism. This certainly is not to say that Arminians as a class deliberately reject the Bible as the Word of God and enthrone human reason in its stead. But it is sadly true that Arminianism denies certain plain teachings of the Word of God because human reason cannot reconcile them with other equally plain teachings of special revelation; and that, too, is a kind of rationalism. For instance, in the interest of human responsibility Arminianism does great violence to the divine sovereignty. In the same manner the Dutch Remonstrants of the first quarter of the seventeenth century, in their zeal to uphold the universal and sincere offer of salvation, denied the truth that God designed by the Saviour's death to save only the elect. These Remonstrants charged that the Reformed teaching of the particular design of the atonement leaves no room for the universal and sincere offer of the gospel. What was Calvinism's answer? It may be said that Arminianism set a trap for it. Said Arminianism in effect: "The limited design of the atonement and the universal and sincere offer of the gospel obviously contradict each other; no thinking man can hold to both; we choose for the latter over against the former, and you Calvinists

18. Pp. 9f.
19. *The Well-Meant Gospel Offer,* p. 78.

have no choice but to reject the latter if you insist on the former." Did the Calvinists of that day walk into this trap? That would have been naive indeed. Had they done that, they would have committed the identical sin of rationalism of which the Remonstrants were guilty. In a word, they would have sacrificed precisely that which is of the very essence of Calvinism. They did nothing of the kind. Instead, they subjected finite and faulty human reason to divine revelation. Admitting its inability to square these two doctrines with each other before the bar of human reason, the Synod of Dort accepted both for the simple and conclusive reason that both are taught unmistakably in Holy Writ. The Canons of Dort insist that "it was the will of God that Christ by the blood of the cross . . . should effectually redeem out of every people, tribe, nation and language all those, and those only, who were from eternity chosen to salvation and given to Him by the Father";[20] but they state just as unequivocally: "As many as are called by the gospel are unfeignedly called. For God has most earnestly and truly declared in His Word what is acceptable to Him; namely, that those who are called should come unto Him."[21]

The Minutes of the Fifteenth General Assembly of the Orthodox Presbyterian Church contain a painstaking exegetical study of the Scriptural warrant for the Reformed doctrine of the universal and sincere offer of salvation.[22] It was prepared by Professors John Murray and Ned B. Stonehouse of Westminster Theological Seminary and was subsequently reprinted in booklet form under the title *The Free Offer of the Gospel.* The passages studied are Matthew 5:44-48; Acts 14:17; Deuteronomy 5:29 and 32:29; Psalm 81:13ff.; Isaiah 48:18; Matthew 23:37; Luke 13:34; Ezekiel 18:23, 32 and 33:11; Isaiah 45:22; and II Peter 3:9. The Scriptural evidence for this doctrine is so overwhelming

20. Second Head of Doctrine, 8.
21. Third and Fourth Heads of Doctrine, 8.
22. Philadelphia, 1948, Appendix, pp. 51-63.

that the limitation of space forbids its detailed presentation in this connection. However, some brief comment on a few of the passages cited seems desirable.

The study referred to might well have quoted Calvin's comment on Ezekiel 18:23, "Have I any pleasure at all that the wicked should die? saith the Lord God: and not that he should return from his ways and live?" Says Calvin: "God desires nothing more earnestly than that those who were perishing and rushing to destruction should return into the way of safety. . . . What the prophet says is very true, that God wills not the death of a sinner, because he meets him of his own accord, and is not only prepared to receive all who fly to his pity, but he calls them towards him with a loud voice, when he sees how they are alienated from all hope of safety . . . . If any should object — then there is no election of God, by which he has predestined a fixed number to salvation, the answer is at hand: the prophet does not here speak of God's secret counsel, but only recalls miserable men from despair, that they may apprehend the hope of pardon, and repent and embrace the offered salvation. If any one again objects — this is making God act with duplicity, the answer is ready, that God always wishes the same thing, though by different ways, and in a manner inscrutable to us. Although, therefore, God's will is simple, yet great variety is involved in it, as far as our senses are concerned. Besides, it is not surprising that our eyes should be blinded by intense light, so that we cannot certainly judge how God wishes all to be saved, and yet has devoted all the reprobate to eternal destruction, and wishes them to perish. While we look now through a glass darkly, we should be content with the measure of our intelligence."[23]

In the Authorized Version of the English Bible, II Peter 3:9 reads: "The Lord is not slack concerning his promise, as some would count slackness: but is longsuffering to us-ward,

23. *Commentaries on the First Twenty Chapters of the Book of the Prophet Ezekiel,* transl. by Thomas Myers, Edinburgh, 1850, *loc. cit.*

not willing that any should perish, but that all should come to repentance." However, there are good reasons for preferring the reading "to you-ward" of the American Revised Version or "toward you" of the Revised Standard Version to the reading "to us-ward." After careful study of this passage, the authors of *The Free Offer of the Gospel* take certain positions, two of which will here be noted. One is that the pronoun designating those toward whom, or on account of whom, God is longsuffering cannot properly be restricted to the elect or to believers. The other is stated thus: "The reason or ground for the longsuffering of God until the day of judgment is given in what is said concerning his 'willing.' He is longsuffering in that, or because, he does not wish that any men should perish, but rather because he wills or wishes that all should come to repentance. Repentance is the condition of life; without repentance men must perish. But the will of God that men be saved expressed here is not conditional. It is not: I will your salvation if you repent, but: I will that you repent and thus be saved. The two clauses then go far beyond defining the longsuffering of God, for they intimate what is back of his longsuffering. This favor is grounded in God himself; it is an expression of his will with regard to sinners, his will being nothing short of their salvation."[24]

At the close of that study the authors summarize their findings. Say they in part: "We found that God reveals himself as not taking pleasure in or desiring the death of those who die but rather as taking pleasure in or desiring the repentance and life of the wicked. This will of God to repentance and salvation is universalized and reveals to us, therefore, that there is in God a benevolent lovingkindness towards the repentance and salvation of even those whom he has not decreed to save. This pleasure, will, desire is expressed in the universal call to repentance."[25]

24. P. 25.
25. Pp. 26f.

Herman Bavinck, that prince of Dutch theologians, says: "Although it is true that through calling salvation becomes the portion of but few, as everybody must admit, yet it has great value and significance also for those who reject it. It is for all without distinction proof of God's infinite love and seals the word that He has no pleasure in the death of the sinner but therein that he live; it declares to all that the sacrifice of Christ is sufficient for the expiation of all sins, that no one is lost because it is not rich or powerful enough."[26] Significantly, Bavinck relates the universal and sincere offer of the gospel to the universal suitableness and sufficiency of the atonement, not to an alleged divine purpose of universal salvation through the atonement. And Charles Hodge asserts: "As God in the course of nature and in the dispensation of his providence, moves on in undisturbed majesty, little concerned at the apparent complication or even inconsistency of one effect or dispensation with another; so the Spirit of God in the Bible unfolds the purposes, truths, and dealings of God, just as they are . . . . On the same page we find the assurance of God's love to sinners, and declarations that He would that all men should come unto Him and live, with explicit assertions that He has determined to leave multitudes to perish in their sins. In like manner, the express declarations that it was the incomprehensible and peculiar love of God for his own people, which induced Him to send his Son for their redemption; that Christ came into the world for that specific object; that He died for his sheep; that He gave Himself for his Church; and that the salvation of all for whom He thus offered Himself is rendered certain by the gift of the Spirit to bring them to faith and repentance, are intermingled with declarations of good-will to all mankind, with offers of salvation to every one who will believe in the Son of God . . . . All we have to do is not to ignore or deny either of these modes of representation, but to open our minds wide enough to receive them both, and reconcile them as

26. *Gereformeerde Dogmatiek,* IV, 7.

best we can. Both are true . . . whether we can see their consistency or not."[27]

Thus appears the utter folly of the popular notion that the Calvinist cannot preach a full gospel for the reason that he cannot tell men that Christ died to save each and every one of them. As Cunningham remarks in his *Historical Theology,* this is "a mode of preaching the gospel never adopted by our Lord and His apostles."[28] What the minister of the gospel needs to tell men is that Christ died for the ungodly (Rom. 5:6), that consequently God makes to the ungodly everywhere a *bona fide* offer of eternal life if they repent. But he may not stop there. He must go on to declare to sinners that God sincerely invites them to repent and believe because He does not desire the death of any but the salvation of all, and that Christ will in no wise cast out any that come to Him. The preacher must be bold to assure sinners, not merely that God will be pleased to save them *if* they repent and believe, but that nothing will please God more, or, as Calvin puts it in his comment on Ezekiel 18:23, that "God desires nothing more earnestly," than that they repent and believe and thus be saved.

Not only does the Calvinist present the universal and sincere offer of the gospel as does the Arminian. The truth is that this offer as made by the Calvinist is incomparably more meaningful than is this offer as made by him who makes salvation dependent on the free will of man. The latter boasts of his "whosoever will" gospel. But what avails it to proclaim a "whosoever will" gospel in a world of universal won't? Yet, if it be left to man to will, that is an accurate description of the world in which we live. One might as well proclaim to the dead in a cemetery: "Whosoever will may arise." The Calvinist, on the other hand, depends not on the will of natural man but on the grace of God Almighty. He knows that in this world of otherwise universal won't

27. *Systematic Theology,* II, 561.
28. II, 344.

there are here and there and everywhere those who by the grace of God will. Thus the "whosoever will" gospel when proclaimed by him becomes meaningful. And it is sure to bring response.

Viewed from still another angle, the universal and sincere offer of salvation as presented by the Calvinist is incomparably richer than is that offer as presented by inconsistent universalism. What does the gospel offer but Christ Himself? More specifically, it offers the Christ crucified. But the crucified Christ of inconsistent universalism, whether Arminian or Barthian, and the crucified Christ of Calvinism are not in every respect identical. In a most important respect they differ. The crucified Christ of the Arminian has done no more than open the road to life eternal; the crucified Christ of the Calvinist has procured eternal life. Consequently the Arminian preacher offers the sinner a so-called chance at salvation, while the Reformed preacher offers him actual salvation. And Barth's Christ, too, cannot unreservedly be depended upon to apply salvation to all whose curse He bore on the cross. The conclusion is warranted that only on the basis of the particularistic view of the divine design of the atonement can the universal and sincere offer of salvation be proclaimed in all its Scriptural fullness.

The Salvation of the World

All too often the salvation wrought by Christ is viewed individualistically only. Christ does indeed save individuals, but by and through the salvation of individuals He saves the world. He who forgets this can never do justice to the universalistic passages of Scripture. Christ is the Saviour of the world. God designed that He should be that, for "the Father sent the Son to be the Saviour of the world" (I John 4:14). "He is the propitiation for our sins; and not for ours only but also for the whole world" (I John 2:2). There is no contradiction in saying that Christ died for His people and that He died for the world. However few or many His people may be today or tomorrow, in the end His people will be the world.

It is of the genius of the Reformed faith to stress this truth, for by virtue of the covenant of grace, which looms so large in the Reformed theology, it is in a position to view the saved organically. The elect are not just so many individuals, but collectively they constitute the church. And men are not so many particles separated from one another as isolated units. On the contrary, they are members of that organism which is known as the human race. Therefore the divine plan of salvation deals not merely with individuals, but with the greater units of which these individuals are the constituent elements. God designed that Christ by His death should purchase His church and should redeem mankind.

It is helpful to remember that the salvation of the world, like the salvation of the individual, is a process. Individuals are saved by stages. Regeneration, conversion and active faith, justification and adoption, sanctification and glorification follow one another. Sanctification is ordinarily a long process. Every saved person on earth still needs to be saved. The best Christian is still an exceedingly poor Christian. Frequently he becomes the prey of temptation and falls into sin. Every once in a while he has to sigh: "The good that I would I do not, but the evil which I would not, that I do" (Rom. 7:19). Not until his last breath will the saint cease to be a sinner. And not until the last trump sounds will his perfected soul and his incorruptible body enter upon the full enjoyment of life eternal. Likewise the salvation of the world is a process. Only gradually and with many interruptions does it proceed to completion. And it is no more reasonable to object to the present incompleteness of the world's salvation than to object to the present incompleteness of our own personal salvation. What concerns us above all else is to rest assured that as, when Christ comes, individual believers will be like Him because they will see Him as He is (I John 3:2), so also at that very time there will come into being a new heaven and a new earth in which will dwell a new humanity (Rev. 21:1). Thus there will be a world that is fully saved. Therefore the Scriptural teaching of the salvation of the world is not universalism in the usual sense of that term. Not everybody will be saved. As in the tedious process of the salvation of the individual much time, many talents, and numerous opportunities are lost, so in the tortuous process of the salvation of the race many men will be lost. But in the former case there will be at last a fully saved individual and in the latter case a fully saved world. As Warfield has said: "This may possibly be expressed by saying that the Scriptures teach an eschatological univeralism, not an each-and-every universalism."[29] Nor does one need to hold to a postmillenarian view of the future, as Warfield did, in order to subscribe to that apt statement.

God designed by the atonement to save the world in an even broader sense. As individual men are members of that organism which is known as the human race, so the human race is an element in the universe. Christ's death has significance for the universe. Origen was of the opinion that Christ suffered meritoriously for inanimate creatures. While there is no Scriptural warrant for that notion, Scripture does teach that, as the fall of man, the head of creation, affected creation adversely, throwing it into disorder, so Christ, who has atoned for the sin of man, will ultimately destroy also this consequence of man's sin. To that Paul referred when he said: "For the earnest expectation of the creature waiteth for the manifestation of the sons of God. For the creature was made subject to vanity, not willingly, but by reason of him who hath subjected the same in hope, because the creature itself also shall be delivered from the bondage of corruption into the glorious liberty of the children of God. For we know that the whole creation groaneth and travaileth in

29. *The Plan of Salvation,* pp. 130f.

pain together until now" (Rom. 8:19-22). Elsewhere Scripture tells us that "in the dispensation of the fulness of times" God will "gather together into one all things in Christ, both which are in heaven and which are on earth," (Eph. 1:10) and that "having made peace through the blood of his cross," God will "reconcile all things unto himself . . . . whether they be things in earth or things in heaven" (Col. 1:20). The view that these passages teach the final restoration of all creatures, even of the fallen angels and the reprobate, is contradicted by the clear teaching of Scripture elsewhere. Bavinck is of the opinion that there is a reference here to the good angels. They were part of the sum total of created angels, and the defection of some could only result in the disorganization of the organism of the angelic host; but in Christ perfect organization will be restored.[30] Be that as it may, the use of the neuter, "all things," is significant. Clearly the reference is to the universe. Sin disturbed and distorted the relationship of all created things both to God and to one another. But in Christ, specifically because of His death which vanquished sin, this consequence of sin will be removed. God will reconcile all things to Himself and bring them into perfect harmony with each other. This is the cosmic significance of the cross of Christ, and it, too, is a significant element in the divine design of the atonement.

Not only does the Reformed theology in fact teach a universal divine design of the atonement, but it may and must be said that only on the basis of the Reformed faith can a true universalism be consistently maintained. The universalism of those who teach that Christ by the atonement designed the ultimate salvation of all men and perhaps of all angels and that this will surely come to pass is indeed an unqualified and in one sense a consistent universalism, but because it is contradicted by Scripture it cannot be rated as a true universalism. It is a figment of the emotional speculation of men. The universalism of those who

30. *Gereformeerde Dogmatiek,* III, 537.

teach that God designed by the atonement to save all men but somehow does not effectively bring that design to complete fruition is neither consistent nor Scriptural. It is a spurious universalism. Calvinism, on the other hand, teaches a truly Scriptural, hence a true, universalism.

What makes the Calvinist a particularist is his insistence on the central teaching of Holy Writ that salvation is from God and from God alone. The very same insistence makes him also a universalist in the Scriptural meaning of that term. The sovereignty of God is the only sure foundation for a living assurance of the salvation of either an individual or the world. "If you wish," says Warfield, "as you lift your eyes to the far horizon of the future, to see looming on the edge of time the glory of a saved world, you can find warrant for so great a vision only in the high principles that it is God and God alone who saves men, that all their salvation is from him, and that in his own good time and way he will bring the world in its entirety to the feet of him whom he has not hesitated to present to our adoring love not merely as the Saviour of our souls, but as the Saviour of the world; and of whom he has himself declared that he has made propitiation not for our sins only, but for the sins of the world. Calvinism thus is the guardian not only of the particularism which assures me that God the Lord is the Saviour of my soul, but equally of the universalism by which I am assured that he is also the true and actual Saviour of the world."[31]

The same erudite and devout divine concludes his precious little volume *The Plan of Salvation* with the telling sentences: "It must be punctually observed that unless it is Christ who, not opens the way of salvation to all, but actually saves his people, there is no reason to believe that there will ever be a saved world. The salvation of the world is absolutely dependent (as is the salvation of the individual soul) on its salvation being the sole work of the Lord Christ himself, in his irre-

31. *The Plan of Salvation*, p. 126.

sistible might. It is only the Calvinist that has warrant to believe in the salvation of the individual or of the world. Both alike rest utterly on the sovereign grace of God. All other ground is shifting sand."[32]

32. *Ibid.*, p. 132.

INDEX OF PROPER NAMES

Anselm of Canterbury, 45
Arminius, Jacobus, 24, 25, 43, 67
Augustine of Hippo, 20, 62, 67, 69

Barth, Karl, 5, 13, 44, 45, 47, 49, 50, 51, 52, 53, 54, 55, 56, 57, 58, 59, 61, 71, 73, 76, 77, 95
Bavinck, Herman, 49, 50, 62, 70, 93, 98
Beckwith, C. A., 25
Beet, Joseph A., 20
Bengel, J. A., 20, 33
Berkhof, Louis, 7, 38, 42, 80, 81, 83, 84
Berkouwer, G. C., 7, 45, 54, 57
Boer, Harry R., 46
Boettner, Loraine, 7, 40
Brunner, Emil, 44
Bultmann, Rudolf, 44

Calvin, John, 8, 33, 47, 51, 62, 66, 69, 81, 82, 83, 91
Candlish, Robert S., 83
Carver, William Owen, 25
Chauncy, Charles, 12
Chillingworth, William, 25
Clarke, Samuel, 25
Clement of Alexandria, 11
Cunningham, William, 83, 94

Daane, James, 81
Dahle, Lars Nielsen, 84
De Jong, A.C., 36, 89
Denney, James, 7
Dodd, C. H., 13

Edwards, Jonathan (elder), 62
Edwards, Jonathan (younger), 20
Erigena, John Scotus, 11

Farmer, H. H., 13
Ferré, Nels F. S., 7, 13

Gregory of Nazianzus, 11
Gregory of Nyssa, 11
Godet, F. L., 20, 33
Greydanus, S., 35
Grosheide, F. W., 29

Hastie, William, 12
Hengstenberg, Ernst W., 33
Hodge, Archibald A., 62, 70
Hodge, Caspar W., 48, 62, 70
Hodge, Charles, 18,19, 21, 22, 62, 67, 68, 70, 78, 79, 93
Hofmann, J. C. K., 20, 21
Holsten, K. C. J., 20

Kittel, Gerhard, 17
Klooster, F. H., 7
Knox, John, 62
Kuiper, Herman, 82
Kuyper, Abraham (Sr.), 62, 70

Luther, Martin, 33, 62, 69

Machen, J. Gresham, 7, 29, 36, 62, 72
Mayhew, Jonathan, 12

Meyer, H. A. W., 19, 20, 33, 35, 60
Michaelis, Wilhelm, 13
Murray, John, 90
Myers, Thomas, 91

Nelson, Horatio, 28
Niebuhr, Reinhold, 44

Olshausen, Herman, 33
Origen, 11, 13, 14, 97
Owen, John, 28, 29, 42, 43, 80

Paterson, William P., 12, 16
Piscator, Johannes, 38
Plato, 11
Pringle, William, 34

Robinson, J. A. T., 13
Rueckert, Leopold I., 20

Schleiermacher, F. W., 11
Shedd, William G. T., 21, 38, 71
Sheldon, Henry C., 75
Smeaton, G., 38
Smith, William, 12
Spurgeon, Charles H., 6, 62
Stonehouse, N. B., 30, 90
Swedenborg, Emanuel, 12

Taylor, Jeremy, 25
Taylor, John, 25
Thayer, Joseph H., 17
Thornwell, James H., 62, 70
Tillich, Paul, 44
Tillotson, John, 25
Turretin, Francis, 37

Van Til, Cornelius, 7, 81, 87, 88
Vos, Geerhardus, 48

Warfield, Benjamin B., 7, 22, 30, 34, 50, 51, 58, 59, 61, 62, 70, 75, 97, 99
Wesley, John, 41, 75
Westcott, B. F., 35
Whitby, Daniel, 25
Whitefield, George, 62
Wycliffe, John, 62

INDEX OF SCRIPTURE PASSAGES

GENESIS
4:20-22 – 82
6:3 – 82
12:3 – 31
18:32 – 82
20:6 – 82

DEUTERONOMY
5:29 –90
32:29 – 90

PSALMS
3:8 – 40
72:8-10 – 31
81:13ff. – 90
86:9 – 31
87 – 31
115:3 – 39
147:19, 20 – 31

ISAIAH
14:24, 27 – 39
45:22 – 90
46:9-11 – 39
46:10 – 22
48:18 – 90
53:7, 8 – 33
53:11 – 66
55:1 – 85

EZEKIEL
3:19 – 85
18:23 – 36, 90, 91, 94
18:32 – 90
33:11 – 36, 90

DANIEL
2:44 – 31
4:35 – 22

JOEL
2:32 – 26

MATTHEW
1:21 – 64
5:13 – 82
5:43-48 – 81-82
5:44-48 – 68, 90
10:22 – 28
11:25, 26 – 60
11:28 – 85
12:32 – 17
13:40-42 – 17
13:48-50 – 17
18:8 – 17
22:14 – 60
23:37 – 85-86, 90
25:41 – 17
25:46 – 17
28:18-20 – 31

MARK
9:44-48 – 16

LUKE
6:33 – 82
12:4, 5 – 16
13:34 – 90
24:46-48 – 31

JOHN
1:29 – 33
3:3 – 27
3:16 – 25, 30
3:36 – 18, 26-27
4:42 – 32-33
6:35 – 41
6:37 – 71
6:39 – 66
6:44 – 41
10:11, 15 – 64
10:18 – 66-67
11:19 – 28
12:20-32 – 31-32
12:28, 29 – 66
14:6 – 26
15:13 – 64, 68-69
17:1-16 – 60
17:4 – 66-67
17:6 – 66
17:9 – 64, 66
17:11 – 66
17:12 – 66

ACTS
1:8 – 31
2:21 – 26
10 – 31
13:48 – 60
14:17 – 90
16:14 – 41

20:28 – 64
26:4 – 28

ROMANS
5 – 45
5:6 – 94
5:8 – 69
5:17 – 21
5:18 – 20, 21
6:1-11 – 45
7:19 – 96
8:11 – 21
8:19-22 – 97-98
8:29 – 48
8:29, 30 – 58, 60
8:30, 32 – 74
8:32 – 64
8:32, 35 – 69
9 – 58, 60
9:16 – 40
9:21 – 60-61
10 – 58
10:11, 13 – 54
11 – 58
11:32 – 21, 34
11:33 – 87
14:15 – 37-38
16:26 – 17

I CORINTHIANS
8:11 –37-38
15:20 – 21
15:22 – 20, 21
15:23 – 21

II CORINTHIANS
5:14, 15 – 72-73
5:15 – 29
5:19 – 14, 36, 45
5:20 – 15

GALATIANS
1:8 – 38

EPHESIANS
1:1-12 – 58, 61
1:4 – 60
1:4, 5 – 67
1:10 – 18, 36, 98
2:8 – 40, 41
2:14, 17 – 31
5:25 – 64

PHILIPPIANS
1:29 – 41
2:12, 13 – 40

COLOSSIANS
1:19, 20 – 18
1:20 – 20, 36, 98
3:11 – 85

II THESSALONIANS
1:8, 9 – 18
1:9 – 17

I TIMOTHY
2:4 – 36
4:10 – 81

II TIMOTHY
1:9 – 17

HEBREWS
2:9-17 – 28-29
2:16 – 18
10:29 – 38

I PETER
1:2 – 48, 61
2:8 – 61

II PETER
2:1 – 38
3:9 – 36, 90, 91-92

I JOHN
2:2 – 25, 26, 35, 36, 95
3:2 – 96-97
3:16 – 69, 73
4:10 – 69
4:14 – 33, 95

JUDE
7 – 17

REVELATION
14:11 – 18
21:1 – 97